What in the World is the World Council of Churches?

An interview
with Philip Potter,
text by Ans J. van der Bent,
and some useful
reference material

World Council of Churches
150 route de Ferney, 1211 Geneva 20, Switzerland

ISBN No. 2 - 8254 - 0582 - 5
Cover design: Paul May
© 1978 World Council of Churches
No. 1 in the Risk book series

Table of contents

I. The WCC's first thirty years

The Rev. Dr Philip Potter, a Methodist minister from Dominica, West Indies, has been general secretary of the World Council of Churches since 1972. Before that he directed the Council's Commission on World Mission and Evangelism. In this interview, he reviews the changes in the Council's life since it began in 1948:

Risk: The ecumenical movement has undergone a sea change during the last 30 years. How would you describe this transformation?

Potter: Well, let's use the image of the ecumenical ship for a start. In the first drawings, you had a choppy sea but the ship was rather solid, riding placidly. Whereas in these last 30 years, there are a lot more people on the ship, there are roughly twice as many churches as there were in 1948. And most of them come from Eastern Europe and the South — Africa, Asia, Latin America, the Caribbean and the Pacific. Then you also had, 30 years ago, the East-West conflict which was balancing itself out. And now this East-West conflict is joined by the North-South conflict, and the East-West conflict is also played out in the South. These things are bound to affect the World Council of Churches.

If you add to that the fact that since Vatican II the Roman Catholic Church has come very firmly within the ecumenical movement, then you see how extensive that sea change has been. For example, I remember the time in the WCC when the issue of religious liberty was defined as the denial by Roman Catholics of such liberty for Protestants in countries like Latin America and by Muslim states against Christians.

Risk: Have these changes made the sea rougher?

Potter: Yes, we are now in choppy waters, if not hurricane seas, and the ship is there, rocking along. But there are certain things that have remained constant, and perhaps the most important thing is the cross, that cross beam which represents the cross in the ecumenical ship. It still is the one point that holds all of us together and it has become very real because we have been forced to carry that cross for and with each other in very concrete terms.

Risk: In trying to identify this sea change more precisely, can you see a shift of ecumenical interest — for example, away from global issues towards more localized (and personalized) questions: racial identity, spirituality, sexuality, and so on?

Potter: It is not a shift of interest. I've seen in these last 30 years that the two things have interacted. As we have faced the global issues we have been forced to see them expressed locally, and we've also found that local issues cannot be solved except in a global perspective. But from whichever end you define the issues, they all need a new spirituality, a new person. As Karl Marx said, if we are to achieve change we need new persons. He spoke here out of his Jewish and Christian background.

My own perception is this: we have had to go through the extremely painful and necessary exercise of discovering that structures, problems, issues, crises are not things in themselves. They are created by persons, and must be understood by persons and dealt with by persons. Therefore the question arises, what kind of persons? Hence, we must bring these structures and institutions, these principalities and powers, back to a sphere of human responsibility. And for that you need new persons.

So the Gospel for me is more alive than ever and people are themselves aware that they need to change their styles of living, their styles of thinking, to experience repentance (*metanoia*), and to recover the sense of a more united courage to face the issues of our time.

Risk: Would you say that has involved a shift from an interest in ecclesiastical issues to a much broader vision of the ecumenical task?
Potter: Well, I don't think the ecumenical movement and the WCC were ever only concerned about ecclesiastical issues. The unity of the church has been and remains the goal. But the unity of the church has never been seen in narrow ecclesiastical terms. There has always been the concern about the church's mission and witness in the world: indeed, some of it came before the movement towards ecclesial unity.

Risk: Where, then, do you see the change in the issues faced by the Council?
Potter: The issues have become much more global and much more concrete. When one looks back at ecumenical statements of even 30 years ago, they seem to be very general, or precise only in terms of the war which had just finished in Europe. But now the issues concern every part of the world, and involve all of us. That's what makes it difficult.

What is more, our analysis of these issues engages us more deeply. For example, we always knew that the church needed repentance and change and so on. But when you start to say precisely how much the churches are actually caught in structures of injustice through their investments and their social and political relationships, that hits us hard.

Take the whole question of participation in society and treating people as subjects, not objects. This has come to us through the women's liberation movement and the youth and student upheavals. But when we start to look at our own hierarchical church structures, and ask how much real participation they afford, then we realize just how much progress we have to make. We're a long way from being the church of the whole people of God, which involves the recognition of every gift and the place of every person in the decision-making and the ministries of the church.

Risk: But isn't there a danger of being so precise about the churches' weaknesses that you begin to offend the member denominations of the WCC? Is there a limit to the awkwardness of the questions that the ecumenical movement's entitled to pose?

Potter: Our faith is a scandal, it's an offence. And if we are to carry out our mission in the world, we become an offence to the world. Jesus did not promise us anything more than the hatred of the world. And we ought to be able to face it because the faith and the church are not ours, they're Christ's. We are the stewards of God's will and purpose. Therefore we should be able to allow the Holy Spirit to guide us together as we face what the world sees as the offence and the scandal. Because it's not a matter of judging each other, but rather of expressing God's judgment on all of us, and therefore being open to his renewing mercy.

Risk: How would you describe the mood of the ecumenical movement in 1978?

Potter: The present mood of the movement lies not in seeing things on a grand scale but in recognizing that in each place people are called into this united courage. And for that they need a spirituality.

Remember that I Corinthians 12 starts with "concerning spiritualities" and goes on to speak about the body and its parts — their integrity and their responsibility one to and for each other.

And the greatest gift of all, *the* gift of the Spirit, is love. Now the most important thing about love that's said in I Corinthians 13 is the capacity to be open to each other and to hang on together, whatever happens. That is the love which abides.

I see this happening in many small groups around the world. These groups become the seedbeds of a new outpouring of God's spirit which will help us to look at each other in new ways and to push our churches into renewed obedience to God's call to the unity of his people. And that includes the recognition of otherness in different cultures, and the richness they can bring in. I find a tremendous thirst for that richness wherever I go.

Risk: In your public statements, you often talk about "the universal dialogue of cultures". This is part of your vision of what the ecumenical movement is about?
Potter: Yes, it is, and it's something, you see, that is in my own personal make-up. I come from an area of the world which is a great mingling of cultures and my Christian faith came out of that background. In our world today, we're coming to recognize that we live in a global village. We talk a great deal of the conflicts which arise the closer we come together, but we haven't talked enough about how much richer our life could be through this intermingling. The discovery and experience of that richness is what I see as the great forward step in the ecumenical movement.

Risk: Isn't there a danger, though, of this universal dialogue of cultures being confined to a relatively privileged strata in the life of churches and society?
Potter: Not in the least. I think one of the things that is happening is that we intellectuals and privileged people have ourselves lost something of the spontaneity and richness that come from this cultural intermingling. We are much like each other, really — a world intellectual elite. We've lost our roots and we're all seeking to recover them. But these roots cannot be confined to one place because they're mixed up all over. And in discovering the richness of that mixture, I think we have extraordinary possibilities ahead of us. It's happening already in art, in music and many other spheres — and it is a counter-attack against the kind of homogenization that science and technology have brought us.

Risk: I've heard you argue that in discovering how other Christians understand the faith, some churches have actually changed the character of their life-style as a result of this ecumenical dialogue. Can you elaborate on that?

Potter: Yes. Take, for example, the last Christian Conference of Asia Assembly. If you look at the reports, they were not as intellectually rich as I have seen in previous meetings. But the meeting itself was much richer than I've ever seen because people were not ashamed to share what they were. Some were very simple, ordinary folk who came to give their testimonies, and their stories held all the richness of the Gospel as it was lived. That's what all of us need to hear — a kind of simplicity and depth which at the same time is extremely complex and tough.

Risk: The last 30 years have seen a gradual reduction in the Western, European influence on the whole direction of the ecumenical movement. You've helped this happen. But has this reduction of a Western character for ecumenism gone far enough?

Potter: Well, I would say the process has gone some way, thanks not only to Third World people but also to people from the North. But for a lot of people it hasn't gone far enough. And both are right. So it has to be a continuous process.

Perhaps in future there won't be so much of this pressure from those of us who come from the Third World about the West or Northern dominance, because in a way none of us is innocent any more. We all share the sinfulness of our situations and we're all in need and we all have something to offer, and I'm hoping that in this new period there will be far more openness to give and receive and less attacking and counter-attacking.

I think we are reaching a period of some synthesis, because right now nobody knows how to go forward. Take the monetary crisis, for example. The Third World now has pretty competent economists of its own, and they can contribute to facing that crisis.

In the same way in the ecumenical movement, there has been a tremendous flowering of theological reflection based on very painful experience in Latin America, among the blacks in North America, in Africa and in Asia. Third World people don't have to have the kind of complex they had before about having to learn all their theology from the North. We hope that our fellow Christians in the North, whether Orthodox or Catholic or Protestant, will be able to open themselves much more with the Third World to God's enriching word.

Risk: Where do you see the ecumenical movement drawing its energy from today?

Potter: Precisely from this increasing engagement of Christians. The fact that we're no longer afraid to be involved, to be soiled. I don't think the churches can be accused as they used to be 30 years ago of being ghettos. That doesn't mean that they have given up some of the ghetto attitudes, but I think they're much more open and more ready to expose themselves to the tempests of our time. And that in itself is a source of energy because it is when we venture out in faith that we know the power of God at work in the world.

Risk: It's become a fashionable debate to draw a distinction between the WCC as an institution and the WCC as a movement. And after 30 years of growth, there are plenty of institutional features. Now there's a kind of yearning in some quarters that looks back to the old days when things were freer and more flexible and decisions could be made more straightforwardly. Do you, as general secretary, share that yearning for a simpler style, and is this tension between institution and movement an accurate one? .

Potter: I think those who have the nostalgia are the people like myself who belong to the old boys' club. We enjoyed this kind of personal relationship, talked the same language and had the field all to ourselves. Now we have to be engaged in action. We have to make our insights and our wisdom happen, and for that you cannot escape institutions. The question is whether the institution is answerable all the time to the insight. The fact that the WCC is under constant attack, and incidentally has changed its structure three or four times in 30 years, means that the movement still has the upper hand with us. You only need to compare us with other international institutions to see that, and we are still a comparatively small body in terms of the whole world of the Christian community. It's a constant struggle.

To Christian intellectuals who aren't engaged in action of some sort, "institution" is always a bad word: it's one of the fashions that we have. But you can't do much without institutions. And by institution I mean the corporate means of moving from one place to another, and seeing that things are done and that what is done is shared elsewhere. You can't just do that by talking and holding the occasional meeting.

Risk: The fact that the Council now has some 300 member bodies must also have institutional implications?

Potter: Yes, because it is equally true that you cannot change locally any more than you can internationally without some form of institution. When you talk about people's movements and people's participation, this cannot happen just by itself. Recently I read that when the Royal Society was formed in England in the 17th century, the founders were told they must stay out of politics and so on. But they formed a society, an institution, and through that means they were able, by their various researches and their organized thought, to go on to organized action. And what an enormous effect they have had on the world! So in these ways, the institution is the servant of action.

Of course, we Christians talk of the incarnation and Jesus Christ took on the form, and *form* is the word, the structure and form of the servant. Now what is it like to be a servant church today? This involves something more than nice spiritual talk. Such a church has to have a shape. The question is what kind of shape, what kind of institution and whether it is an institution that's flexible enough to be responsive to change in order to do what needs to be done.

Risk: Thirty years on, though, there are still large parts of the world church that, even if they've heard of the WCC, really don't know very much about it. There's been a curious reluctance to recognize what the WCC has stood for. What are some of the obstacles that prevent the ecumenical movement and the way that God moves in it from being properly recognized? Is it simply a lack of effective publicity on the ecumenical movement's part?

Potter: Oh, yes: there's always the problem of communication. Even the churches, for all their structures and their authority, can't always understand in their own local expressions what's going on nationally. So we'll always have that problem.

And any reform, any movement for change would always be in a minority, hidden away, because people don't want to change, they don't want to know: that's part of life. There is also the fact that through the ecumenical movement we have been forced to think much more clearly, sharply and radically about the nature of faith and its expression in action. And most of our churches have not been able to cope with that. Faith and action, except for personal morals which the churches can handle almost legislatively, have always been difficult for them, and there are all the political, historical and other reasons for that.

So how do you enable Christians to make their faith happen, not just in personal family terms but in all the concrete realities and conflicts in which they live? That's one of the major tasks ahead of us. There is also an element in the World Council that it must live with, and that is that many of the best things we do cannot be reported and should not be. Therefore there will always be a certain agnosticism around the Council. But far more important, I think, is that the ecumenical movement should not be seen just in terms of a body called the World Council. The

Council's task is to enable the church in each place to be the ecumenical movement.

Risk: Your own personal involvement with the World Council spans its full 30 years. Looking back, what are the moments you remember with the greatest pride and satisfaction?
Potter: I think the most important highlight is that these churches which had for centuries been separate from and in conflict with each other have been able to live together and indeed deepen and widen the fellowship. Today, they face much more clearly and much more fiercely the conflicts which divided them in the past. They have been able to do this and also maintain the fellowship and strengthen it. I think this has been the great miracle.

When I, for example, as a West Indian (and in my own family, half Roman Catholic and half Protestant), went to the last Assembly of the Caribbean Conference of Churches, which is made up of Catholics and Protestants, it was difficult to distinguish between the two. The kind of fellowship we enjoyed there, the kind of struggles we were able to have that cut across our confessions in the context of prayer and celebration, was indeed a great miracle of God for all of us.

I would also say that the Bible has become alive for us in an extraordinary way through these years. We started with it as the heart and centre of the ecumenical movement — the rediscovery of the Bible, its unity, its diversity, the whole prophetic tradition and so on. Thirty years ago we understood this intellectually but the ways in which we have been living it and the kinds of theologies that we have to focus on — the theology of liberation, black theology, the theology of hope in Europe, and the theology of hope and suffering in Asia — these are all biblically centred. While in Cuba recently I was intrigued to find Christians who had given themselves totally in the struggle for socialist society now centre their life on this study of the Bible as it speaks to their situation.

And what's fascinating, too, is the way in which new songs, new prayers, new liturgies are springing up through all these encounters of the Word of God with the struggles of people. This has been one of the great blessings of these years.

I remember in 1948 when we young people had a separate assembly, we were sitting behind the platform, leading the singing and looking at these rather venerable delegates down below.

Their average age was about sixty at that Assembly and there were very few women. Today the ecumenical movement has brought together the whole human family — the wide spectrum of races, cultures, sexes, age groups and so on. Of course, it's still partial, but it's been a very real development and to have participated in that has been a great joy.

I would also say that one of the most significant things we have learnt in these years has been to learn from all the disciplines, the intellectual disciplines — science, technology, art and literature, the lot. From all these and the people involved in them, we have been able to gain a much richer understanding of our world.

Another exciting development has been to discover anew our own responsibility as human beings for our world and the fact that the decisions lie with us — change lies with us and not in some general ideas and ideologies. This humanizing of our world has been one of the significant gains of these years. Of course it brings the travail much closer because the responsibility is frightening. Hence the recent talk of spirituality, not so much for combat, but in combat. This has become much more natural for us to perceive and accept.

There was a time not long ago when we rejected the traditional spiritualities and felt that we could go out and engage ourselves fully in the struggle. We even talked about secular ecumenism. Well, we found that secular ecumenism is right, in the sense that we were in time and in space. But the time and the space drain us, they empty us, and unless we are constantly being renewed by the resources which God supplies, we cannot carry on. That discovery is bringing to the fore the rich resources that our churches have in each place. And on that level, we are all more willing to learn from each other than on the level of cerebral, intellectual confessions and expressions that we have produced. That has been a great gain.

Risk: What are the points of entry for people who stand outside the Christian church to the process you've just been describing?
Potter: I don't think it's so much a point of entry for them but it's a point of entry for us. This is the true evangelistic task, to share the good news that those people outside the church you refer to are accepted. To offer this kind of meeting in the life of the world is, I think, one of the great excitements of our time.

We don't have to go to the world and tell them how different we Christians are. All we need to do is to go in our integrity. The rest will speak for itself.

Risk: You talk about highlights and excitements over the last 30 years. What about the pain and disappointments?
Potter: We have sometimes made wrong-handed decisions for which we had to pay the price. We have, in the midst of conflict, sometimes hurt people one way or the other and we have had to learn how to be more patient — but patient in an impatient way, if you see what I mean.

I think sometimes we have thrown the baby out with the bathwater. Take the period in the sixties when Christians said, we must go out as an exodus people. Then when things got rough, they said we were in exile and all that. Some people refused to join the exodus, then afterwards said, I told you so. Now that kind of pain has not been easy for us to live with. We have had to experience very ferocious attacks and misrepresentation and things of that sort. But I think we've come out of it tested by fire, and there's a lot of fire yet to come.

Risk: Looking ahead, what do you see as issues likely to preoccupy the ecumenical movement?

Potter: I think the crunch for us is on two levels. One concerns the just society in which there is participation by all, in which we are able to sustain the resources of creation for the benefit of all. This involves the new international economic order, transnational corporations, human rights, the militarism issue, the role of science and technology and all that — extremely tough issues, which engage us right to the core of our existence. They're going to create a great deal of conflict, and yet we have to deal with these issues head on because we are now in the midst of it and we can't opt out of it.

And for doing that we need secondly to discover the tremendous reality and power of the various Christian communities in each place which are all part of the whole worldwide community.

Now that sounds easy, but it's not, because two things are happening at the same time in our world. Whether we like it or not, we are sucked into this world community. On the other hand, our reaction is to assert the local setting. There is a right insight in that reaction but there is a great danger. We need to make opportunities out of being both local and global. That is the task before us. In terms of the church it's to discover what it means to be the universal church in each place, in communion with the churches around the world. It also involves this universal dialogue of cultures that I talk about, which is much more than people normally mean by the word "culture"; it is the sharing of all that we are and have. And to be in the midst we need to discover the tremendous reality and power of the Christian community, as part of the worldwide community of peoples.

Risk: To attempt those tasks as we enter an economic climate that is less than welcoming, and where the pressure on resources is increasing — doesn't that discourage you?

Potter: No, not really. Naturally there are headaches to face, but it's amazing how many other resources there are that are untapped. Take just a simple thing. During the war there were many parts of the world where missionaries and money were no longer available. Yet after the war when missionaries went back to those places they found the church had grown and some other leaders had emerged whom nobody had thought about before. Sometimes we have limited our resources far too much to the conventional. This period before us is an opportunity to discover new resources, human ones especially, with the discernment and in the fellowship of love.

Risk: So even after the World Council's 30 years of building up an institutional shape and forming a history, I hear you asking for the movement to retain a capacity to be surprised.
Potter: If it ceases to be surprised it will cease to be, because surprise is an expression of God's opening hope before us, calling us forward, and the moment we cease to be that then we'll cease to move.

II. Before and after 1948

BEFORE 1948

When Martin Luther pinned his Ninety-Five Theses to the door of Wittenberg Cathedral in 1517, he had no idea that the solid stem of the church he challenged would soon be split into a thousand branches. Reforming the church in Geneva, John Calvin was unable to see the schism ahead between the Church of England and Rome in 1570. Still less could he foresee the formation of Congregational, Baptist and Methodist churches in Great Britain, let alone Mennonites, Brethren, Disciples of Christ, Old Catholic churches in Europe and North America.

But the divisions in the church had begun long before Luther. Five centuries before the Reformation a first great schism between Greek and Latin churches had already taken place. From 1054 onward Eastern churches continued to celebrate the divine liturgy according to the Byzantine rite and rejected the authority of the Pope in Rome. Orthodoxy became a self-contained world of its own and almost nine hundred years were to pass before Western theologians began to take serious notice of Orthodox theology. Only after World War II did churches in the West start to care about the life of millions of Orthodox Christians in the socialist countries.

In fact church concern of any sort that crossed denominational lines was in short supply. Until the beginning of this century,

Martin Luther, 1483-1546 (front left), Philipp Melanchton, 1497-1560 (front right), and other reformers. Painting by Lucas Cranach. (Unless otherwise indicated, copyright on all photographs is held by the WCC. Photos available from WCC Film and Visual Arts Department, P.O. Box 66, 1211 Geneva 20, Switzerland.)

John Calvin (1509-1564) addressing the City Council of Geneva

nearly all Christian churches lived in self-centred isolation. Each church, small or large, pointed to its own tradition, celebrated its own liturgy, shepherded the needs of its own flock and was preoccupied with its own identity. The idea of churches together rendering witness and a service to the world was foreign. Theology was carried on in the form of confessional monologues. The individuals that dared to talk about the church of Jesus Christ as one family, with a common history and a common destiny, were classified as utopian and odd, or simply ignored.

The church's habit of branching out (and breaking off) in all directions wasn't simply a European matter. Divisions were soon transplanted in mission lands, from the 17th century onwards, as the growth of European colonies and church expansion went hand in hand. After the founding of the Baptist Missionary Society in 1792 and the London Missionary Society in 1795 many other national denominations and free churches followed suit by creating their own missionary agencies. As at home the First Presbyterian Church stood next to the First Baptist Church and opposite the Second Methodist Church in the same street of the city, so mission posts and new churches were created next to one another in numerous places in Asia, Africa and Latin America. There were a few exceptions: J. H. Taylor, for example, founder of the China Inland Mission, was resolutely non-denominational by refusing connections with any one particular church.

The birth of the ecumenical movement

By the beginning of the 20th century, Christianity was a genuinely international religion and had decisively broken out of its

Western boundaries. Missionaries had created schools and colleges, championed native people in fights against white exploitation, played an important role in the legal abolition of slavery, pioneered medical services, helped to check cannibalism and infanticide, and made notable translations of the Bible; through all this they had contributed to the transformation of countless lives by the power of Jesus Christ. However, the patterns of teaching, catechizing and including the new faithful in each local denominational church were the same; regardless of the culture, the unspoken assumption was that Western standards of literate faith were the norm. Not only was there often a sharp rejection of indigenous culture wherever it impinged on religion, but the converted natives had to conform strictly to the tradition, doctrines and ethical standards of each mother church engaged in the missionary enterprise. Even today, John Wesley's most precise disciples are found as frequently among Polynesian Methodists in the South Pacific as they are among English Methodists on Wesley's home territory.

World Missionary Conference, Edinburgh, 1910

Slowly but ever more deeply the disgrace of disunity has been felt. It was the missionary expansion, notably in Africa and Asia, which gave birth to the 20th century ecumenical movement. This movement is generally reckoned to have begun at the World Missionary Conference at Edinburgh in 1910. The event had been preceded by the formation of various transdenominational bodies during the 19th century, in particular the Evangelical Alliance (1846) — dedicated to promoting the interests of a "Scriptural Christianity", the oppressed religious minorities in the West and the observance of an annual week of prayer — and the World Student Christian Federation (1895), formed to draw together the student Christian movements in various countries. Two of the principal architects of the Edinburgh Conference were John R. Mott and J. H. Oldham who, together with one of the ushers, William Temple, later Archbishop of Canterbury, were destined to play at a later stage a leading role in the formation of the World Council of Churches.

Archbishop William Temple (1881-1944) addressing a Convocation at Canterbury

John Mott (1865-1955), an American Methodist, was secretary of the International Committee of the YMCA and general secretary of the World Student Christian Federation. An imposing figure in stetson hat and cutaway coat, he remains known chiefly for his zealous propaganda on behalf of missions, based upon the watchword "The Evangelization of the World in our Generation". Joseph Oldham (1874-1969) was a British Anglican layman and undoubtedly the greatest pioneer of the 20th century ecumenical movement. He was a shy, short man who pursued the ecumenical

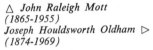

△ *John Raleigh Mott*
(1865-1955)
Joseph Houldsworth Oldham ▷
(1874-1969)

cause with a widely respected tenacity. Like Mott, he too worked as secretary of the Student Christian Movement and the YMCA. From 1921-1938 he was the soul of the International Missionary Council and also became the chief architect of many important ecumenical gatherings, in particular the very carefully prepared Second World Conference on Church and State at Oxford in 1937. The reports of this conference fill eight thick volumes.

The Edinburgh Conference led to the International Missionary Council in 1921, created "to help coordinate the activities of the national missionary organizations of the different countries and to unite Christian forces of the world in seeking justice in international and inter-racial relations". To achieve this lofty goal a whole series of world missionary conferences followed. From 1939 onwards the International Missionary Council worked closely with the World Council of Churches (while the latter was "in process of formation"). Then in 1961, after the Third Assembly in New Delhi, the Missionary Council became the Division of World Mission and Evangelism of the WCC. It had taken several decades to realize that the unity of the church and the mission of the church are but two sides of the same coin. The *International Review of Mission*, the major organ of the ecumenical missionary movement since 1912, is still published today in the Ecumenical Centre in Geneva.

Bishop Charles Henry Brent
(1862-1929)

Archbishop Nathan Söderblom
(1866-1931)

"Service unites, doctrine divides"

The ecumenical movement as it developed flowed through two other streams of international Christian endeavour. Bishop Charles Brent, an American Episcopalian who attended the

First World Conference on Faith and Order, Lausanne, 1927

Edinburgh Conference, launched a proposal for a conference on Faith and Order to include representatives of "all Christian communions throughout the world which confess the Lord Jesus Christ as God and Saviour". The first fully constituted World Conference on Faith and Order took place at Lausanne in 1927, only two years before Brent's death, but other meetings followed, at Edinburgh (1937), Lund (1952) and Montreal (1963). All these Faith and Order gatherings were not only concerned with ways of organic church union but also with seeking together a common mind on various matters of Christian theology, tradition and renewal. From the very beginning numerous discussions took place on whether the Faith and Order movement sought a federation of independent churches, based on doctrinal compromise, or whether it should tackle something more innovative and far-reaching.

The third channel of 20th century ecumenism had a service aspect and was of great ethical significance. This movement came to be known as Life and Work and it was decisively influenced by Archbishop Nathan Söderblom of Sweden. Famous as a scholar in the field of comparative religion, he outgrew the rationalism of the liberal era, while preserving the positive values of

sound critical scholarship. His enthusiasm for Christian unity, kindled in his youth, made him another outstanding leader of the ecumenical movement. In 1925 on his initiative the Universal Christian Conference on Life and Work was convened at Stockholm in order to study the application of Christian principles to international relations and to social, industrial and economic life.

The movement went forward under the slogan "Service unites, doctrine divides" and hence in its early stages avoided too much discussion of a doctrinal nature. The report of the Oxford Life and Work Conference (1937) remains to this day the most comprehensive ecumenical statement on problems of church and society and Christian social responsibility. It was the impetus of this Life and Work movement that helped develop the ecumenical quest for a responsible world community expressed so often in WCC gatherings since 1948. This quest had often led to controversy. The Third World Conference on Church and Society, for example, held in Geneva in 1966 and involving 400 lay experts and theologians, saw a sharp confrontation of the technological expertise of the Western industrialized world with the revolutionary politics of the Third World, particularly Latin America.

The road opens up

It soon became evident that if the churches were to give adequate support to the ecumenical cause, both Faith and Order and Life and Work (and later World Mission and Evangelism) ought to join together in a single movement. A provisional committee, meeting at Utrecht in 1938, laid the first solid foundation on which the permanent structure of the World Council of Churches was built over the next two decades. The most important constitutional questions concerned the authority and the basis of the Council. There is no doubt, however, that the disastrous effects of World War II determined the main course of the ecumenical movement. In spite of the isolation and hatred of nations many churches remained in contact through the Geneva office, under the able leadership of W. A. Visser 't Hooft, the general secretary of the Council. Chaplaincy service, work amongst prisoners of war, preparation for Christian reconstruction after the war and the reconciliation with the Evangelical Church in Germany constituted a vital contribution to the supra-national witness of the church.

The words: "We intend to stay together" provided a moving testimony from all representatives participating in the First

Assembly of the World Council of Churches in Amsterdam, 1948. Never before had so many Christians from so many different traditions and backgrounds prayed the Lord's Prayer together, everyone in his or her own language. Never before had there been such a shared enthusiasm and conviction among Anglicans, Baptists, Congregationalists, Calvinists and Lutherans, Methodists, Mennonites, Quakers, Moravians, Disciples, Old Catholics, the Salvation Army and a number of the Orthodox Church. The Church of Jesus Christ was finally marching on the road to visible unity, empowered to give a joint witness and engaged in a common service to the world.

And it was Dr Visser 't Hooft who helped to launch this journey. Born in 1900 in the Netherlands he, like so many other ecumenical leaders, began his career as secretary of the World Alliance of YMCA's (1924-1931) and as general secretary of the World Student Christian Federation (1931-1938). In 1938 he became general secretary of the World Council of Churches, at that time "in process of formation". Occupying that post until his retirement in 1966 he almost single-handedly directed the work of the Council, presided over countless meetings, travelled widely throughout the whole world, was the architect of the first official contacts with the Orthodox churches and the Roman Catholic

Dr Willem Adolf Visser 't Hooft, first general secretary of the World Council

Church and the author of an impressive collection of books and articles on ecumenical themes. His memoirs, published in 1973, span the experiences of a man who has been immersed in and shaped by international ecumenical life for more than fifty years.

AFTER 1948

With its first assembly, held in Amsterdam in 1948, the World Council of Churches began a growing process that 30 years later shows no signs of stopping. Nor does the chain of conferences and consultations — ever more numerous and ambitious in their undertakings. The WCC assemblies, especially, have become more and more formidable affairs requiring at least three years of intensive preparation. At the Fifth Assembly at Nairobi in 1975 there were almost 3,000 people, including delegates, consultants, observers, visitors and a press corps large enough to stage a conference of its own.

The variety of churches and Christians gathered in the Council is ever more unlimited. Quakers worshipping in silence and Orthodox churches celebrating their exuberant divine liturgy seem worlds apart. Salvationists singing hymns in the slums seem to have very little in common with the Old Catholics' emphasis on the mystical Body of Christ. The Church of Christ on Earth begun by the prophet Simon Kimbangu in Zaire, not recognizing the sacraments of baptism and the eucharist, can hardly be compared with the Lutheran Church of Sweden. But churches not only differ in confessional and theological positions. Some have millions of members, others only a few thousands. Some Christian communities live and witness in authoritarian states of the political left or the political right. Many are burdened with the problem of affluence, others live among the poorest of the poor. Yet all these churches attach great value to a place in the ecumenical fellowship. In Amsterdam, 1948, 146 churches officially constituted the World Council of Churches. At that time only 30 churches came from Asia, Africa and Latin America. Today almost 300 churches from every continent, First World, Second and Third, are members of the Council.

That impressive membership is no chance collection. It reflects a growing trust in the Council as an agent of Christian unity and action. This brief sampling of highlights since 1948

First Assembly of the World Council of Churches, Amsterdam, 1948: Communion service   ▷

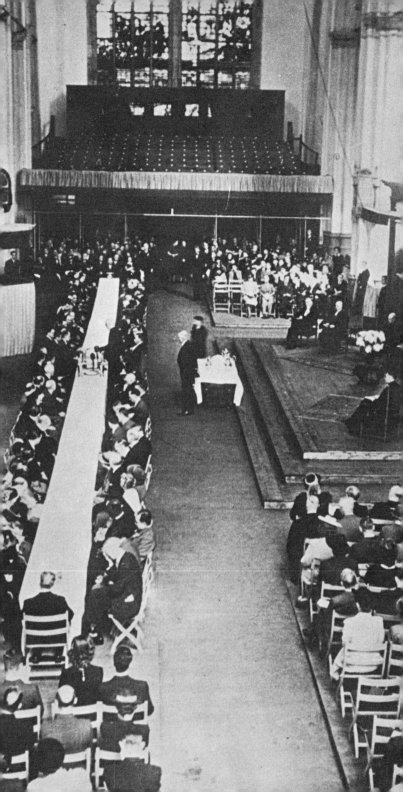

serves only to illustrate the breadth and complexity of the Council's history over these last three decades. Let's begin, then, with the second WCC Assembly at Evanston in 1954 which reflected many of the tensions of the Cold War rampant at the time. It was not accidental that the assembly's theme was: "Jesus Christ the Hope of the World". Delegates resolved to dedicate themselves to God anew, "that He may enable us to grow together".

Two years before Evanston, the Third World Conference on Faith and Order at Lund was largely concerned with clarifying the differences that existed between churches and comparing the traditions out of which these differences had emerged. The aim of the Lund report was "to penetrate behind the divisions of the church on earth to our common faith in the one Lord". The phrase "non-theological factors" commanded increasing attention as it was realized that not only questions of doctrine but social, political and cultural factors played their part in dividing the churches.

The Third Assembly at New Delhi in 1961 was marked by several new major events. The 20th century missionary movement became fully integrated in the Council's concerns. After long deliberations the Orthodox churches in the socialist countries joined the World Council.

In the Fourth World Conference on Faith and Order at Montreal in 1963 the full effect of Orthodox participation and the presence of Roman Catholic observers in the theological discussion was felt. Thorny questions of Scripture, tradition, worship, unity and the nature of ministry were tackled.

The main shift of emphasis illustrated at the World Council's Division of World Mission and Evangelism meeting in Mexico City (1963) carried with it a new insight into the nature of the church's missionary task. *Mission to Six Continents* was the title of the published report. The assumption that the Western world itself no longer needed to be evangelized was radically challenged. All continents need to receive the Gospel anew and to come to terms with its demands and promises.

In 1966 the World Conference on Church and Society was held in Geneva. Concentrating on such concrete issues as world economics, development, responsible participation in political life and structures of international cooperation, the conference had a great impact on the Fourth Assembly at Uppsala in 1968.

More than other assemblies, the Uppsala gathering faced squarely the conflicts of this world: the growing gap between rich and poor nations, the disastrous effects of white racism, the ambiguity of new scientific discoveries, the tensions between generations and the student revolts. Youth participants in great numbers were very articulate and frequently critical of what went on in the sessions.

The triennial meeting of the Faith and Order Commission at Louvain in 1971 had different concerns. It dealt with a number of ongoing studies on such subjects as baptism, confirmation and the eucharist, ordination, worship, and the nature of scriptural authority. All these were received alongside the main theme, "The Unity of the Church and the Unity of Mankind".

And in the same year as the Louvain meeting, in Lima, Peru, ten years of conversations ended with the integration into the Council of two important ecumenical organizations — the World Council of Christian Education and the World Sunday School Association.

The Commission on World Mission and Evangelism Conference at Bangkok (1972-73) on "Salvation Today" was another landmark meeting. It refused to separate the human being into

Fifth Assembly of the World Council, Nairobi, 1975

Pope Paul VI visiting the World Council, 1969

body and soul or to resolve the tension between personal and social aspects of salvation. Though this position gave rise to misunderstanding and criticism, the meeting brought new insight into the comprehensiveness of God's will for the salvation of all humankind in all its cultural diversity. The WCC's Fifth Assembly, meeting in Nairobi in 1975, showed that the ecumenical movement had reached a new level of maturity. At the World Council's most representative gathering ever assembled, an impressive range of issues were covered with a degree of understanding few observers had thought possible. The list of the six sections into which that Assembly's main business was divided illustrates something of the ambitious scope of the meeting: Confessing Christ Today; What Unity Requires; Seeking Community — the Common Search of People of Various Faiths, Cultures and Ideologies; Education for Liberation and Community; Structures of Injustice and Struggles for Liberation; and Human Development — the Ambiguities of Power, Technology and Quality of Life.

The Roman Catholic Church

For all its ecumenical service over the last 30 years, the World Council of Churches is not itself the ecumenical movement.

Other forces and other churches, in particular the Roman Catholic Church, not yet belonging to the World Council, also strive for the unity of all Christians. Roman Catholicism has radically changed its attitude towards the ecumenical movement during the last 20 years. The decisive turning point came with the Second Vatican Council and the great influence of Pope John XXIII. Before that time the official position of the Vatican was negative towards rapprochement with other churches. In 1961 Rome at last agreed to the participation of official observers in the New Delhi Assembly, while in return a great number of delegated observers from various denominations were invited to attend the Vatican Council. The Council's Decree on Ecumenism praised "the ecumenical sincerity and energy of the separated brethren". Pope John XXIII created in 1960 a Secretariat for the Promotion of Christian Unity which coordinates all ecumenical relations with non-Roman Catholic churches. Cardinal Augustin Bea was named its first president, and Monsignor Jan Willebrands its first secretary. From 1965 onwards a Joint Working Group — its members are appointed by the Vatican Secretariat for Christian Unity and the World Council of Churches — has met annually to discuss common problems and concerns among their members.

But collaboration goes much further. The Committee on Society, Development and Peace (SODEPAX), appointed jointly by the Pontifical Commission Justice and Peace and the World Council, continues its activities. The Week of Prayer for Christian Unity is annually prepared by a group of World Council and Roman Catholic representatives. The Faith and Order Commission now includes a considerable number of Roman Catholic members. For more than a decade now, any important World Council conference or consultation has been attended by a number of official and fully participating Roman Catholic delegates. In addition there are ad hoc contacts in regard to many programmes and projects of common interest. It was with this spirit of cooperation in mind that Pope Paul VI, visiting the World Council at Geneva in 1969, called the occasion "a prophetic moment and truly blessed encounter".

Yet for all that, it remains extremely difficult to remove remaining obstacles on the road to doctrinal agreement and visibly restored unity. The eventual membership of the Roman Catholic Church in the World Council of Churches is still a wide open question. Because of its hierarchical structure and its sheer numerical weight, the Roman Catholic Church would create a whole series of new administrative and psychological problems, not to mention the theological ones, if it entered the World Council as a full member. Its membership, in fact, would require a change in the Council's constitution, alter the Council's character and create an entirely new situation. Whatever the ultimate shape of the greater unity the churches seek to manifest — many Christians pray for a eucharistic unity of all in each place — it will certainly not be any expansion or imitation of the kind of unity currently existing within the Roman Catholic Church. This largest Christian community, as it freely acknowledges, is also called to radical renewal, like the rest of the Christian denominations.

Other ecumenical bodies

Besides the Geneva based World Council of Churches, there are numerous national and regional ecumenical bodies, many of them associated with the WCC. Among the older Christian councils are the National Council of the Churches of Christ in the United States of America (1950), the British Council of Churches (1942), the National Christian Council of India (1947) and the Christian Council of Asia (formerly the East Asia Christian Conference, 1959). They all have similar aims and functions as the World Council of Churches. The Roman Catholic Church has become a full member of more than 20 national councils of churches and also of the Caribbean and Pacific regional councils.

There are also 12 international confessional organs of which the Lutheran World Federation, the World Alliance of Reformed Churches and the World Methodist Council have their offices with the WCC in the Ecumenical Centre in Geneva. The Centre also provides offices to the Conference of European Churches, and representatives of the Russian Orthodox Church and the Ecumenical Patriarchate in Constantinople.

In addition to all these bodies, there are almost 200 ecumenical institutes around the world with a variety of programmes. European ecumenical institutes have made scholarly contributions to ecumenical theology, social ethics and spirituality, while Asian and African study centres have deepened the understanding of the Christian faith in a multi-religious environment.

But it is probably on the very local level that the ecumenical movement has progressed more than anywhere else. Joint catechetical classes are conducted by Roman Catholic priests and

Protestant ministers. Mixed-marriage groups are alive and actively reminding the respective ecclesiastical hierarchies of their pastoral responsibilities. Ecumenical baptisms and marriages are ever more frequently celebrated. New church buildings serve several denominations under one roof. Ecumenical groups share everything from Bible study to sponsorship of a development project in a Third World country.

This all goes considerably beyond the once-in-a-year coming together for the Week of Prayer for Christian unity and an occasional exchange of pulpits. That sort of ecumenism is now seen as old and timid. Hesitant church authorities cannot slow down any more the pace of ecumenism, precisely because too many local congregations have joined the march.

New forms of Christian fellowship

The ecumenical movement is still further propelled by less formalized Christian communities and groups, trying out spontaneous or experimental forms of worship, common life and witness, and social action. Protesting against the complacency of the institutional churches and the bureaucracy of their ecumenical organs, these groups often provide a creative challenge to traditional church life and *status quo* ecumenical attitudes. The variety of these groups is enormous, as this sampling shows.

More than four centuries after Luther's attack on monastic vows, the first Protestant Taizé brothers said their regular "offices" together in the cathedral of St Peter in Geneva where Calvin (who also condemned the monastic life) had preached. The brothers' life of prayer, which sustains their life of service, has not been a mere imitation of the ancient monastic centres, such as Cluny, although this historic site lies near Taizé in Burgundy. When the *Office de Taizé* was published in 1962, its careful balance of old and new aroused the attention of many who were concerned for the renewal of Christian worship. The establishment of this charitable and liturgical community has challenged Protestants and Catholics together to reconsider their past rejection of each other. Hundreds of thousands of young people have made a pilgrimage to Taizé and celebrated the eucharist with the brothers, all of whom have all taken the traditional vows of life-long poverty, chastity and obedience.

Evangelical academies and lay training centres provide another challenge to established ecumenism. The work in these places has been formed not so much around the traditional order of common prayer or the free worship of Spirit-filled groups of believers, as around the contemporary disorder of life in the world. These academies and centres were born in Germany as a result of ruin in the 1940's. The academies of Bad Boll, Arnoldshain, Loccum, Tutzing, the Sigtuna Foundation above Lake Mälar in Sweden, the Kerk and Wereld Institute at Driebergen near Utrecht, and several other communities, have been effective in meeting people's spiritual and intellectual needs, running conference retreats, specializing in courses for politicians and trade unionists, discussing the life problems of industrial workers and training lay workers for parishes and schools. Lay institutes have spread outside Europe, in Japan, Korea, India, Zambia, Australia, Canada, the United States and many other countries. They have all helped to bring a renewed Christianity to grips with the secular world.

In France, radically minded Christians responded to their country's political drama back in 1939 by creating the CIMADE *(Comité Inter-Mouvements auprès des Evacués)*. Old people, the chronically unemployed, discharged prisoners, foreign students and thousands of migrant workers have been given friendship and some security by the workers of this two-thirds French, one-third international volunteer organization.

In the Shalom movement in the Netherlands, Catholic and Protestant young people, laity and clergy have been cooperating in projects related to the renewal of the Church ("the small oikoumene") and the peace and development of the world ("the large oikoumene").

In Agape and Riesi, two centres in North Italy and Sicily respectively, the work centred around Tullio Vinay has aroused the interest and respect of Christians and non-Christians worldwide, as a sign of a new desire in the churches in Western Europe to identify themselves with the young and the poor both at home and abroad.

And in West Germany, the *Kirchentag* every two years brings Christians together in their tens of thousands for several days of intensive education and argument. These rallies, which make special provision for many international visitors, owed their existence to the vision and courage of one man, the late Reinhold von Thadden-Trieglaff. The *Kirchentag* has crossed the political barriers dividing Germany. Collaboration with Roman Catholics has grown. The massive efficiency and success of the rallies continue to attract many ecumenical visitors, and provide a meeting point for German Christians from the East and the West.

The growth of Pentecostalism has been phenomenal during the past few decades. Its manifestations — speaking in tongues *(glossolalia)*, divine healing and prophecy — are parts of a charismatic revival which has affected all the traditional Protestant and Roman Catholic churches in Europe, North and South America. Attaching great value to the simplicity and fervour of the Acts of the Apostles, the strength of Pentecostal communities lies in the warmth of their worship. They are in this sense ecumenical, believing that the baptism of the Holy Spirit is available to believers in all ages. A number of Pentecostal churches have joined the World Council of Churches, and some of their leaders have shared in WCC meetings. But there are still many Pentecostal groups which remain suspicious of the official ecumenical movement.

It is still unclear how all these new forms of Christian fellowship have affected the churches around the world. Such terms as "renewal", "radical change", and "revolutionary commitment" prove elusive when it comes to surveys of ecumenism. Various new initiatives have been domesticated by official acceptance. Others wear their unorthodoxy with pride. Many lay people and pastors ask whether renewal can come, but the call to the churches by the First Assembly of the World Council of Churches nevertheless remains valid: "Our first and deepest need is not new organization, but the renewal, or rather the rebirth, of the actual churches." There is indeed an intimate relation between unity and renewal. The greatest contribution to unity will be made by the church in each place and in all places which is most ready to let itself be thoroughly renewed by the Holy Spirit.

III. The way it works

Some visitors to the Ecumenical Centre in Geneva expect to be received in large impressive buildings, similar to the Vatican State in Rome. They soon discover that the headquarters of the World Council of Churches look much like any modern office building — a functional concrete structure four stories high, inconspicuous among the other organizations located in Geneva's "international area".

On a slight rise above the United Nations, the World Health building, and the new headquarters of the International Labour Office, the buildings of the Centre house the Council. The main block with three wings consists primarily of offices in which some 275 people on the Council staff work each day from 8.30 a.m. to 5 p.m. The complex, surrounded by trees, lawns and car parks, also contains a chapel in which staff meet weekly for worship, and daily for intercessions on behalf of the churches. There is also an exhibition and conference hall, smaller meeting rooms, a bookshop, cafeteria and library.

Visitors are many and frequent: they come from all parts of the globe seeking first-hand contact with the Council. A comprehensive programme is often arranged for them, during which staff members interpret the WCC's aims and programmes. In 1977 3,000 people came to the Ecumenical Centre in groups, as well as some 300 individually.

Before moving to the present building in 1964, the Council was located in a chalet and wooden barracks on the other side of Geneva. It was a place for pioneers but became overcrowded as the staff rapidly grew to keep pace with the increasing responsibilities assigned to the Council by member churches. Today, with a large staff and a building already in need of extension, those who remember the days of a smaller, simpler Council wonder where this expansion will end.

Coordinating the work of the programme units and giving leadership to the World Council as a whole is the task of the general secretary, a post presently held by Dr Philip A. Potter, a Methodist from the Caribbean. Participation in the Second World Youth Conference at Oslo in 1947 and the First Assembly of the World Council in 1948 helped to form Philip Potter's passion for the ecumenical movement. He became overseas secretary of the British Student Christian Movement from 1948 to 1950, and he was chairman of the World Student Christian Federation from 1960 to 1968. The general secretaryship is his third assignment with the World Council of Churches: he previously served in the Youth Department as its director, and then headed up the Commission on World Mission and Evangelism.

As general secretary Philip Potter's responsibility is to implement the policies laid down by the churches. These policies are determined by the delegates of the member churches meeting in Assembly, normally every seven years. More detailed decisions are taken by a Central Committee, now of 134 members, elected by the Assembly and meeting annually. The Central Committee in turn appoints a smaller Executive Committee. It also nominates a number of commissions and working groups whose members have special expertise and guide the various programmes. This means that, in addition to the members of the Central and Executive Committees, some 250 men and 75 women from a large cross section of the membership of the WCC are regularly involved in planning, overseeing and implementing the Council's programmes and activities.

Membership

The World Council of Churches "is a fellowship of churches which confess the Lord Jesus Christ as God and Saviour according to the Scriptures and therefore seek to fulfil together their common calling to the glory of the one God, Father, Son and Holy Spirit".

The Council is nothing more: not a universal authority controlling what Christians should believe and do; but also nothing less by now than nearly 300 churches of widely varying traditions and cultural backgrounds, worshipping in hundreds of languages, living under every kind of political order and disorder, and yet committing themselves to sail through the storms of contemporary history in the same boat.

Membership is open to any church which can accept the basis of the World Council, stated above. This basis is not a full confession of faith but rather a foundation for the Council defining its nature and clarifying the limits of its membership. Since the World Council of Churches is not itself a church, it passes no judgment upon the sincerity with which member churches accept the basis. The member churches themselves must remind each other that membership is meaningless if commitment to the basis disappears. The main elements of the WCC's basis are the confession of the Lordship of Christ, fellowship of the member churches, acceptance of biblical authority, common witness and service, and the worship of the Trinity. Some very conservative churches judge the basis not biblical enough; some liberal churches do not accept the trinitarian formula. The World Council nevertheless represents most Reformation and Orthodox churches which together claim 400 million faithful. But how seriously this vast number take their membership in the world body is not a matter that can be legislated. As Archbishop William Temple said: "Any authority the Council will have will consist in the weight which it carries with the churches by its own wisdom."

Structures and programmes

The present divisions and departments of the World Council of Churches date back to 1971 when a three-programme unit structure was formed comprising: Faith and Witness, Justice and Service, and Education and Renewal. The 1971 restructuring aimed to make a more effective use of staff and resources, to operate more efficiently, and to programme priorities more clearly. But the Committee that made the changes emphasized that the work of restructuring is never completed, nor ever will be if the World Council is to continue "to function as a dynamic and ever-

Dr Eugene Carlson Blake, second general secretary of the World Council

changing body". It stated clearly that "there is no one right structure and no theology of structure", that the problem of continuity and discontinuity can never be solved as the Council continues to evolve.

Faith and Witness

Since the unity of the church and the content and manner of the witness of its faith in the modern world are still major concerns of the World Council, Faith and Order, World Mission and Evangelism, Church and Society, Theological Education and Dialogue have been grouped as sub-units of Programme Unit I. The *Faith and Order* Commission's concern is the visible unity of the church. It studies doctrinal and theological issues which still divide the churches and seeks ways to give common expression to the Christian faith. In many places, study groups are working to produce "accounts of Christian hope". Significant agreement has been reached by the Commission on baptism, the eucharist and the ministry; the statements on these subjects are now being revised in consultation with the member churches. The Commission also explores the ways and modes of teaching in the churches, with special emphasis on the reception of ecumenical agreements by the churches. The Faith and Order Commission includes Roman Catholic members.

World Mission and Evangelism assists the Christian community in the proclamation of the Gospel of Jesus Christ, by word and deed, to the world to the end that all may believe in him and be saved. This means sharing information about how churches are fulfilling their evangelistic task, asking what is the mark of a truly missionary congregation, and persuading churches in all parts of the world to share their resources for mission, whether they be people, ideas or money. *Church and Society* at present focuses on the significance of the Christian faith in a world of science and technology. Ethical issues in relation to nuclear power, genetics, and environment have been given special attention. One central question is: how do the rich nations move from their present unjust overconsumption of limited natural resources to a society which is more just, where people are able to participate in decision-making and where creation is conserved and enhanced for the well-being of all, including the poor countries and future generations?

Now to the other sub-units in Programme Unit I. *Dialogue with People of Living Faiths and Ideologies* helps Christians to take their neighbours seriously to build bridges of understanding through conversations with Jews, Buddhists, Hindus, Muslims, Marxists and others. The experience of dialogue and reflection on issues raised stimulates deeper understanding and encourages the search for community. *Theological Education*, the newest sub-unit, replaces the Theological Education Fund and draws on its 20 years of experience. It seeks to cooperate with the churches in their efforts to equip people for ministry and mission on every continent through theological schools and alternative programmes.

Justice and Service

The title of Unit II highlights the crucial importance of the concerns for justice and service within the ecumenical movement. It signifies the common commitment of the member churches to promote social, racial, economic and political justice within and among nations and to provide services to victims of injustice, oppression and poverty to meet their basic needs and to support their struggle for fundamental rights and human development.

Five sub-units work as follows. *Inter-Church Aid, Refugee and World Service* enables the churches to serve each other and to grow ecumenically as they share their resources for service. Each year some $35 million in cash and kind are channelled through the WCC for programmes of human welfare and development in more than 80 countries in response to the needs indicated by the churches on the spot. Included in the flow of resources are help for scholarships, medical care, assistance to churches in minority situations, victims of human rights violations and those caught up in natural and man-made disasters. Refugees, constantly created by war, disaster, political upheaval and persecution, are another ever-present demand on the WCC and the member churches on every continent.

Churches' Participation in Development means concern for social justice at all levels of human existence. Development aims at economic growth, social justice and self-reliance and it can only be achieved through people's participation. Christian engagement requires not just aid but real solidarity with the poor in their struggles. The Ecumenical Development Fund channels money from those churches which have made 2% of their regular funds available for development to support people's efforts against poverty and for justice. Development education, research activities, technical services are tools through which the ecumenical movement tries to assist the churches in their work of solidarity with the poor. In addition, the Ecumenical Development Co-operative Society (incorporated as an independent entity in the Netherlands) makes church investment capital available as low-interest loans to development schemes drawn up by people.

The sub-unit on *International Affairs* is an instrument for Christian witness amid the world's conflicts. By calling the churches' attention to the causes of particular conflicts, to the violation of human rights in particular places and to the evils of militarism, and by being available to represent the churches' concern in areas of tension, it stimulates Christians to work for the healing of the nations, through peace and reconciliation. Racism has been condemned repeatedly as incompatible with the Gospel. Words, however, were not enough, and in 1969 the WCC Central Committee established a *Programme to Combat Racism* to help the churches turn their shared convictions into common actions. The Programme works mainly through a project list, research and publications, as well as a Special Fund supporting organizations of the racially oppressed and support groups in all parts of the world. (Grants in the amount of $2.5 million were made up to the end of 1977.)

The *Christian Medical Commission* emphasizes community health care with the accent on people's involvement in their own care as part of total development, and as a way of meeting health needs of large sections of the world's population so far deprived of health services. It helps church-related hospitals, Protestant and Roman Catholic, join forces with government agencies in this endeavour. Through *SODEPAX*, the joint WCC/Vatican Committee on Society, Development and Peace, the WCC and its members work with the Roman Catholic Church. The present SODEPAX programme, "In Search of a New Society", encourages ecumenical reflection and action at the local and national levels on questions of international social justice, peace and human rights.

Education and Renewal

Programme Unit III has a threefold purpose: to stimulate rethinking about Christian education, to help make the ecumenical movement a reality at the parish level, and to increase participation of women, youth and other lay people in both church and society. *Education* touches most Christians one way or another. "Theological education for the whole people of God", Christian and general education are the three main concerns of this sub-unit. An expert on biblical studies trains Bible study enablers for the churches, a scholarship programme furthers leadership development, problems of family life and childhood are studied, and help is given with the reshaping of church educational curricula. Other high priorities are church educational institutions, the church and the child, and ecumenical education.

Renewal and Congregational Life exists to help local congregations be vital centres of Christian worship, life, mission and service. Through contacts with congregations and other Christian groups and movements, it seeks signs of renewal to share with the churches. *Women* are breaking out of traditional, subordinate roles in their churches as well as in the wider society. This sub-unit challenges the WCC and its member churches to enable

*The World Council's
Geneva headquarters are
housed in the Ecumenical
Centre, a place of
many moods and faces*

women's participation in the full life of the Christian community and society. Its emphases include: education of women for participation, a study exploring theological perspectives on such participation; a programme responding to the needs of rural women; programmes responding to human rights issues and the concerns of such marginalized groups of women as migrants, refugees, domestic workers. *Youth* aims at stimulating young people to explore and live out the Christian faith, and to participate fully in the life of the whole church and the work of the WCC. The sub-unit is building up contacts with young Christians around the world to enable them to bring their concerns and challenges into the central life of the WCC, and pressing for full involvement of youth in all the Council's programmes.

General Secretariat

There are four sub-units directly related to the General Secretariat. The *Communication Department* informs the churches and the wider public about the work of the WCC and assists them to communicate with one another. Press releases, a weekly news service, a monthly magazine, quarterly periodicals, books, photos, films and cassette recordings help keep the churches informed, provide a platform for their news and views, and aid interpretation of the ecumenical movement. The department also works closely with religious and secular media. Though translators and interpreters aid communication across language barriers, the language problem will never be solved satisfactorily. English, French and German are the three operational languages of the Council; at larger conferences Spanish and Russian are added. The participants from the Third World rightly claim that Swahili, Indonesian, Chinese and various other languages should be spoken also; English and French are secondary languages for them and seriously limit their mode of expression. Delegates to meetings may use other languages, provided they follow the Apostle Paul's advice to those "speaking in tongues" — to provide a translation. The technical problems of widespread simultaneous translation and translation of documents in more than five languages remain insurmountable.

The *Finance Department* is responsible for the finances of the World Council — a task complicated by inflation, currency changes and the thousand different financial operations required daily by an international organization. The Council's *Ecumenical*

Institute at Bossey, near Geneva, has provided for more than
thirty years leadership training for Christians from diverse backgrounds. Some sixty students from many countries attend annually a Graduate School semester from October to February.
The *Library of the Ecumenical Centre* holds an extensive collection
of books and papers relating to the ecumenical movement as well
as a large and unique collection of the 20th century ecumenical
and the World Council's own archives. The Library is open to
any student, professor, pastor, priest or lay-person in the world.
Already well over three hundred doctoral dissertations on ecumenical subjects have been written. A *New York Office* of the
World Council maintains relationships with the US member
churches and provides information and study materials.

Budget

The World Council's total budget mirrors its many activities.
Each year the equivalent of over $50 million flows through its
books, including some $35 million en route to other destinations
to help victims of human and man-made disasters and to support
projects ranging from leadership training scholarships to evangelistic activities to rural development schemes and disaster relief.
The rest pays for the World Council's own operations and programmes, both for the programmes of all the sections of the WCC
and for the central administration. It is thus clear that most of the
available money goes to various projects of charity, aid, mutual
assistance throughout the world, while only a small part of the
budget covers the costs of running the Geneva-based headquarters.
Actually, the Justice and Service Unit which includes the Commission on Inter-Church Aid, Refugee and World Service and the
Commission on the Churches' Participation in Development, uses
43% of the $15 million available for salaries and administration.
Besides Inter-Church Aid, Refugee and World Service, the Commission on World Mission and Evangelism has a separate supporting constituency of over 40 affiliated councils and various missionary societies.

Main contributors are the World Council's member churches
and their mission and aid agencies, with some funds for particular projects coming from secular and government organizations
and foundations. There is no fixed membership fee; churches
contribute what they feel they can. This means that, while the
richer parts of the Council's constituency account for a large slice

of its income, churches in the poorer countries also bear part of the cost. Any Christian who is informed about the very large total annual budgets of the national denominational churches in the USA, Great Britain, the Federal Republic of Germany, the Scandinavian and other Western countries, knows that the total annual expenditures of the WCC represent only a very small percentage of the yearly spending of one single church.

Staff

Visitors frequently ask how the Council hires its staff. There is no fixed pattern. As soon as an executive position becomes vacant, member churches and Central Committee members are notified and requested to submit names of candidates. The process of selecting and nominating a qualified person is sometimes complicated. A balanced denominational and geographical representation has always to be kept in mind. At present, staff represents 42 different countries and still many more churches and Christian traditions. The total number of some 275 people

The chapel of the Ecumenical Centre

serving the Council includes programme, technical, administrative and secretarial staff with the most varied educational and professional backgrounds. Many staff members spend a considerable part of their time during a given year on visits to member churches around the world. There is hardly a country that is not visited at least once in the course of 12 months.

With a team as varied and as transient as the Council's staff, regular periods of common worship become an important source of fellowship and a focus of mutual thought. Throughout the week, colleagues gather every morning to offer intercessions for particular member churches, for situations of conflict and need around the world, and for the concerns of the staff community in the Ecumenical Centre. Every week is begun with a fuller service of worship which once a month takes the form of a eucharistic liturgy following the order of one of the member churches of the Council. The search for a new spirituality finds expression in retreats as well as acts of common liturgical celebration, in private prayer and Bible study groups as well as meetings where new hymns from many churches and cultures are sung. Obviously, it is impossible to satisfy the spiritual and devotional needs of every single staff person. But growing together in worship and liturgy is an essential dimension of the ecumenical pilgrimage.

The *oikoumene*, in whatever place and circumstance, merely follows in the footsteps of its Master. Thus also the staff of the World Council is able to accept with joy and in expectation both the challenges and the frustrations, the achievements and the shortcomings, of any study or action programme.

IV. From here to where?

We have briefly described the history of the 20th century ecumenical movement and introduced the activities of the World Council of Churches. But what is at stake for the movement now and what are the prospects ahead? These are hard questions and it would harm rather than promote the cause and the mission of Christ's community on earth to affirm too easily that the ecumenical movement does have a future and that nothing will hinder its course. Already in the first chapter of our booklet the general secretary of the World Council has pointed to the fact that the ecumenical ship is rocking today in heavier seas than it faced at the start of its voyage. And more conflicts, struggles and contradictions will be faced. There are no grounds for simplistic hope in the advance of justice around the world or in the Christian churches as agents for that justice. We go on inflicting suffering on each other individually and through the structures of our societies. Those who enjoy privilege and power fight to keep the *status quo*. Ecumenical efforts to change those vested interests, inside or outside the churches, have to fight against enormous odds. What makes the task so difficult?

Participation and communication

It's easy enough to list the 293 member churches that form the World Council, but who really belongs to the ecumenical movement? Dr Visser 't Hooft has observed that the ecumenical enterprise resembles too much "an army with many generals and officers, but with too few soldiers". Still today the ecumenical movement is not sufficiently rooted in the life of local churches and groups.

"It is clear", said Dr Visser 't Hooft, "that real advance towards full unity will be made only if in the coming years local congregations and their members discover that to follow Christ means to follow him in his work of the building on the one Body, his Body." The intentions of the World Council have been clear from the beginning. Already at the founding assembly at Amsterdam it was noted that "the laity constitutes more than 99% of the church" and that "the churches are too much dominated by ecclesiastical officialdom, clergy or lay, instead of giving vigorous expression to the full rights of the living congregation". And ever since Amsterdam, it has been repeated that it is not enough to secure for the laity some larger place or recognition in the church. Much more is involved, for the ministry of the laity

involves the rediscovery of the true nature of the church itself as
God's people. Lay Christians are everywhere in a much better
position than clergy to provide a two-way communication channel
between church and world. But recognition of that fact is still
slow in coming.

The World Council of Churches has frequently been criticized
for failing to inject its ideas and concerns into local church life
and to stimulate wide participation. Numerous conferences and
group discussions have covered this subject, often ending in
frustration. One thing is quite sure. The process of building
ecumenical awareness is not a matter of internationally tested
techniques or of an enormous centralized department of information. Communication from the Geneva headquarters stops
short at national denominational offices and desks of church
officials. Information from "above" simply doesn't trickle down.
Grass-roots ecumenism won't flourish unless numerous parishes
and local Christian groups spell out for themselves what it really
means to be caught up in the renewed life of Christ's universal
church and a costly participation in its tasks.

In 1977 the World Council's Commission on Faith and Order
published a book entitled *In Each Place: Towards a Fellowship of*

Salgado Junior

Local Churches Truly United. What precisely are the churches looking for when they reflect on and pray for the unity of "all in each place"? No single Christian community has the answer. A cooperative response is required, so it is therefore a real step forward when the WCC's Commission on Faith and Order together with the sub-unit on Renewal and Congregational Life, in cooperation with the Vatican Secretariat for Promoting Christian Unity in Rome, the Lutheran World Federation and the World Alliance of Reformed Churches, have agreed to issue an ecumenical prayer calender: "For All God's People." In this ecumenical prayer cycle an Anglican church in Birmingham, England, can give thanks for the witness of a Baptist church in Seoul, Korea; a Reformed church in Budapest can ask for God's blessing on the Uniting Church in Sydney, Australia; the Coptic Orthodox Church in Cairo is able to intercede for the trials of the Evangelical Lutherans in Santiago, and the Roman Catholic Church in Washington, DC, can share its concern for the Union of Evangelical Christian Baptists in Moscow.

The need of each Christian in his or her own place to be sustained by the prayers of fellow Christians in other places is obvious. The blessing upon those who intercede for others needs no comment. Since the worldwide ecumenical prayer cycle has now started, perhaps also the recent secular custom of towns and cities becoming twin communities with settlements of similar size somewhere else in the world could be adopted for Christian use. The affluent churches in Frankfurt, Federal Republic of Germany, could practise their solidarity with poor Christian communities in Dacca, Bangladesh and the United Church of Christ in Manila, the Philippines, could share its political concerns with the Methodist Church in Belfast, Northern Ireland.

UNITY, MISSION, SERVICE

Yet all this is but the beginning of Christian unity. For there is more to the ecumenical movement than developing a profound sense of the universal Christian fellowship in worship and intercession. Even more deeply at stake is the awareness in Birmingham, Seoul, Budapest, Sydney, Cairo, Santiago, Washington, DC and Moscow, that God in Christ is healing the wounds and diseases of humankind and bringing nations and people to their ultimate fulfilment.

50

In this context, what do unity, mission and service imply, remembering that each one of the three elements cannot be faced alone. There is no secret about the World Council of Churches' struggle to make of its sub-units on Faith and Order, Mission and Evangelism, Church and Society and Dialogue with People of Other Faiths and Ideologies, one coherent and interdependent operation. The frequent embarrassment and inability on the "local level" to speak about faith, witness and political commitment in one breath corresponds to the inability at the Council's level to avoid compartmentalizing its work.

"That the world may believe"

To begin with, unity can never be an end in itself. Jesus prayed that all may be one *in order that the world may believe*. To use a specific example: the matter of intercommunion and shared eucharist is still much debated. Apart from theological divisions and complications there are other hindrances to celebrating the Lord's supper together. Protestants sometimes feel that Roman Catholics deal with the elements as if they had some magical qualities. Catholics, on the other hand, can be shocked by what

Salgado Junior

they judge to be irreverence by Protestants. They also are suspicious of churches that rarely, if ever, celebrate the eucharist at all.

However, as important as the ongoing discussion on the theology and the practice of the eucharist is, it should never become *the* essential and exclusive ecumenical issue. Christians who have not faithfully witnessed and rendered their hard service to their Lord in the world cannot celebrate the Lord's Supper without being suspected of belonging to an introvert and self-righteous people. Jesus clearly says that reconciliation with one's brother is necessary before gifts are brought and offered to the altar (Matt. 5: 23-24).

And if unity and eucharists are not ends in themselves, neither is evangelism. Zeal to win souls for Christ writes its own narrow Christian history if these souls don't go on to witness to the liberated life of the worldwide Christian family, obedient to Christ's command to love one's neighbour as oneself. Liberation has become a ringing catch-word in the ecumenical movement for more than a decade now. Numerous theologies of liberation have been written. The gospel undoubtedly liberates individuals from the prisons of wickedness, aimlessness, fear and despair. But the same offer of liberation is so total that it liberates the church from tending to become an ecclesiastical entity in itself, from the fancy of evangelizing for its own sake, and from the conviction that God cannot handle this world without the social activism of Christians.

Unity, witness and service cannot be properly conceived of, finally, without taking people of other living faiths and secular convictions seriously and eliminating prejudice towards them. Many Christians still feel that mission and dialogue exclude each other, that dialogue is a betrayal of mission and will lead to a new syncretistic world religion. They cannot comprehend that the very word "mission" often includes a threat and an offence to men and women of other faiths and cultures. The term can, indeed, suggest dominance and insensitivity, rather than sharing an understanding of love and responding to the truth. Dialogue is not a matter of swopping concepts and definitions, but of learning to live in community, open to the faith (and practice) of others without being any less committed to one's own belief. Dialogue in this way is always the prerequisite and the setting for proclaiming God's saving power in Jesus Christ. It is the style with which we invite others to participate in this redeeming power.

Holding contradictions together

It is quite likely that the reader of this chapter will irritatedly interject that all that has been said so far is rather remote from the life of a local congregation. Ordinary church life on Sunday morning and during the week seems to have little to do with the lofty ecumenical description of unity, mission, dialogue and service, inter-related as they are. The reality of local church life is less reassuring.

So Roman Catholics, Anglicans and Protestants in Washington, DC, can pray together for true unity, but their timetables for confronting the racism and oppression that sustain the slum areas of their city do not yet coincide.

Christians in Seoul, Korea, courageously continue their evangelistic campaigns in spite of a dictatorial government that interprets their call to submit to the reign of Christ as subversive interference in state affairs. But because of the multi-denominational planting of the gospel in Korea there is still apathy and reticence about joining ranks in a national movement that would replace confessional rivalries with common witness of splinter-churches.

In Santiago, Chile, before the coup against Allende, the churches prayed for liberation from totalitarianism and communism. Now those same churches are thrown back on "spiritual neutrality" and "political abstention". Their very survival is put at stake if they dare to speak out on the violation of human rights in their nation.

Christians in Birmingham, England, know something about empty churches in a polluted, industrial city and the gospel's relevance in strikes and disputes between labour unions and government. Yet they have not made much progress in recog-

nizing the full human and religious rights of migrant Muslim workers and dialoguing with them on reasons that unite and divide their monotheistic faith.

Orthodox believers in Moscow continue to celebrate with fervour and in great joy Christ's victorious resurrection from the dead; their divine liturgy puts up a silent but stout resistance against state harassment and atheistic propaganda. But they are often forced to reduce their faith to a private affair in no relation to society and responsible state citizenship.

Faced with that sort of evidence, is the ecumenical advance among the Christian rank and file throughout the world not a deceiving slogan and a pious dream? Is the common Christian faith deep enough and strong enough to cope with its inability and frequent failure to be at the same time a royal priesthood, a holy nation, God's own people, a Samaritan to the robbed and

Ken Thompson

down-trodden, a Greek to the Greek and a Jew to the Jew? Confronted with questions like these, the ecumenical movement might be expected to lose heart and momentum. Yet somehow it continues to move and hold faith with its future. For ecumenism exists by holding contradictions together. The movement knows all too well that some of its members have a vision of a new social order, some are articulate ambassadors of Christ in a Buddhist, Marxist or Muslim environment, some focus on intensive liturgical and spiritual development, but that all together in the world's eyes the churches still present a rather incoherent global community.

But for all the evidence of frustration and failure the ecumenical movement still manages to plant the seeds of a promise that catches the imagination and excitement of Christians everywhere. The excitement stems from discovering that it is exactly in the midst of grappling with the frustration and despair of the search for unity, justice and peace that God reveals himself most vividly. Churches with a taste of the ecumenical vision are finding that the more they learn about Christ's incarnation and suffering in the world, the more they come to know about resurrection, praise and glory.

V. Misgivings about the WCC

Question: Does the World Council really need to handle a budget of $50 million and employ a staff of 275 people? Even though it began spontaneously as a movement that challenged the denominational church establishment, hasn't the Council itself become an establishment? Has ecumenism let itself become institutionalized?
Answer: It's true that the Council now employs five times as many staff as it did in the early years after 1948, and that it has developed an institutional style of life and work of its own. There is also no doubt that the World Council of Churches conducts all its business meetings in a Western parliamentary style. With its stress on representative democracy, the Anglo-Saxon parliamentary system is a procedure suited to bringing about an agreement on delicate matters where no unanimous decision can be reached. The Council, inasmuch as it is a council of separated churches, is necessarily dependent upon institutional structures which can produce consensus statements. Much work is done through policy reference, nominations, credentials, finance committees and still other committees, with all the complicated procedural operations that that involves.

Dr Visser 't Hooft answers the charge of "institutionalism" very clearly. "Obviously the World Council has institutional features," he says, "but these are not necessarily signs of degeneracy. The World Council has to be an institution in order to do its job. Without a constitution, without common rules, without committees, without a staff, without a budget, all sorts of things can be started but without these things the movement cannot advance and cannot assume a form sufficiently firm to enable it to help the churches to understand their ecumenical responsibility and to achieve a common witness and action in society.

"If we want the end, we must also want the means to achieve that end. If our purpose is to help the churches to achieve a life of genuine solidarity and fellowship, of mutual stimulus and creativity, of practical cooperation, then we must also be prepared to create the necessary network of instruments to keep this process of common life moving. If we want an ecumenical movement which is not just a pious dream but really enters into man's ordinary, everyday life, then we must also seek to make it visible and palpable enough to be taken seriously as a party to the dialogue in the interplay of the forces which actually shape the world in which we live."

Question: Doesn't the World Council's very existence, let alone its activity, encourage a theological conformity?

Answer: The World Council of Churches is neither a monolithic body aiming at regulating the denominations nor an ecclesiastical United Nations. In fact, it's impossible to speak of a single "theology of the Council" as such. Its constituency represents a great variety of confessional traditions, as well as theological trends which cut across denominational lines. All its activities, conferences, consultations, programmes, projects and publications, are directed towards encouraging an ever new and creative encounter between these different expressions of faith. When these ecumenical conversations result in a consensus, it is expressed in the form of official reports or statements addressed *to* the churches or the world at large, but such statements always result from a process of confrontation of widely diverse convictions. In this way, theological agreements and social actions become part of the teaching of the churches themselves, rather than forming an all-round ecumenical theology and a binding ecumenical social ethics.

Question: The World Council involves Roman Catholics in its programme and on its committees and has formal links with the Vatican Secretariat for Promoting Christian Unity. Is the World Council striving towards a world church at the expense of the concern for truth ?

Answer: Compromise is not in the nature of the relationship between Geneva and Rome. It's rather a process of building mutual trust and respect. Thanks to a growing ecumenical spirit, Roman Catholics and Protestants can engage in common worship and shared service. The days of winning converts from each other are over and even if disagreements on central doctrines remain, these differences are not used to avoid cooperation in other fields, such as education, medical care, aid, development and so on.

But the search for unity is not simply a matter of closing a gap between Protestants and Roman Catholics. Within the world Council fellowship, that gap is already straddled by traditions such as the Anglican. The fellowship also includes the ancient churches of Eastern Orthodoxy which have helped to bring a new appreciation for Protestants of the liturgical and sacramental riches in the Christian tradition. To see Roman Catholicism as a separate influence yet to be felt is to miss seeing the catholicity and theological diversity already present in the ecumenical movement.

None of this is to gloss over the failure so far to reach any kind of visible and organized union between Catholic, Protestant and Orthodox churches alike. The problem still is how to relate the right kind of diversity to the right kind of unity, and exactly how the WCC, as a council of autonomous churches, could relate in formal and institutional terms to the centralized authority of the Vatican is an issue that has barely been formulated, let alone studied in depth. Says Dr Alan Brash, recently retired deputy general secretary of the WCC: "Whatever the ultimate shape of the greater unity the churches seek to manifest — and we pray for a eucharistic unity of all in each place — it will certainly not be any expansion or imitation of the kind of unity currently existing within the Roman Catholic Church. That church, as it freely acknowledges, is called to radical renewal, like the rest of our denominations."

Question: What about the charge that the World Council is communist-inspired and controlled?
Answer: The Eastern European churches that form about 13% of the Council's membership would have good cause to wonder at this question. They could claim in reply that the capitalist world is the real controller of the Council. North American and Western European churches form 33% of the total membership.

The fact is that neither argument holds true, for there are tensions between church and state (however differently expressed) on both sides of the communism-capitalism divide. An Orthodox church in the USSR would resent its position being explained away in terms of communist ideology, just as much as a Baptist church in the US would bridle at being described as a rationale for capitalism.

The fellowship of faith and spiritual purpose represented in the Council can't be reduced to the level of political conspiracies by either side. What's more, those who most frequently cry "communist" at the WCC conveniently overlook the fact that the Council can probably claim to have helped more refugees fleeing from communism than any other organization. This is taken for granted by the Western media — who make so much capital out of the fact that the WCC also serves people of socialist convictions fleeing from the torture chambers of fascist states.

The story of primitive anti-communism and anti-communist crusades in the Christian church is a long and sad one. A flood of literature has been written on "how to resist and to fight communism", but good, educational material on "how to encounter anti-communism" in church circles hardly exists. Still today, a great number of Christians facing the communist nations do not question for a moment their superior wisdom and better insight into human nature and all world affairs. They don't begin to understand the honest and deep-rooted anti-religious feelings of many militant communists, who can no longer believe that the Christian churches are engaged in the struggle for social and economic justice. Even those who admit that Marxists at some point rightly criticized Christian civilization are convinced that now, having learned a few good lessons and corrected some mistakes in Western liberal society, they are outside the reach of their attacks and can continue to live on their own behalf.

The World Council of Churches continues to face the tremendous task of promoting the dialogue with people of other ideologies (as well as other faiths) in its worldwide constituency. Knowing that it is impossible to combine faith in God and in Christ as Saviour with the tenets of dialectical and historical materialism, it nevertheless has to call for encounters which foster a broader understanding of the enormous problems of human development faced by all nations, including communist ones. The Council's task remains to serve as a reconciling factor between seemingly irreconcilable standpoints.

Question: Isn't it true that ecumenism, while it grew out of the missionary movement, has become increasingly secular in character? Socio-political concerns seem to have replaced spiritual ones. The horizontal dimension of the cross dominates, the vertical aim is forgotten.

Answer: It is true that particularly during and after the World Council's Fourth Assembly at Uppsala in 1968, ecumenical programmes to combat racism and further peoples' development and human rights have been strongly emphasized. Unit II of the WCC, "Justice and Service", has become the largest in the whole Council's structure of operations.

It is also true, however, that during the Fifth Assembly at Nairobi in 1975 the issue of "horizontalism" was not mentioned any more. On the contrary, to the astonishment of a great number of participants, the assembly sessions refused to separate faith from social action, witness to Christ from political involvement. The call for a new spirituality and a more effectively evangelistic life-style and the call to accept the challenges of burning world issues went hand in hand. Change of heart and change of socio-political structures, Christians in Nairobi asserted, belong together. Significantly, even the controversial Programme to Combat Racism was accepted as part of that social/spiritual harmony. The identification with the poor and the oppressed, delegates emphasized, is closely related to the witness of the suffering, dying and resurrected Lord.

To play up one arm of the cross, over against the other, is a theological tactic now discredited in the face of the Council's commitment to bringing the whole gospel to the whole person.

Emilio Castro, director of the WCC's Commission on World Mission and Evangelism, puts the relation between socio-political and spiritual-evangelical concerns like this: "If the struggle for human dignity comes out of a Christian community that is faithful to the biblical tradition and shows its belief in Jesus Christ in daily life, then the message of that struggle for human dignity will be easily understood. The very life of the Christian community will be a pointer towards Jesus Christ. But we must also say that every evangelistic effort that doesn't share in the human struggle for a decent life and dignity is not good news and is not evangelistic at all." Dr Castro goes on to talk about the churches he's seen, "that after taking a clear stand on the human rights issue, are becoming centres of attraction for the people and are obliged to explain the sense of their commitment. I see the evangelistic attraction of the liturgical life of churches in socialist countries. I see a clear evangelistic message in the prophetic denunciation by black churches in Southern Africa. I see Christians in Western society struggling for a new life-style and showing signs of the Kingdom...

"What really thrills me is to see the Holy Spirit at work, opening doors, releasing our imagination to discover where he is present, calling us to join with him, to discern his name. Some of the most beautiful pages of the churches' history are being written right now."

Appendices

APPENDIX I: ESTIMATED MEMBERSHIP
OF THE PRINCIPAL RELIGIONS OF THE WORLD

RELIGIONS	NORTH AMERICA	SOUTH AMERICA	EUROPE
Total Christian	231,099,700	158,980,000	348,059,300
Roman Catholic	131,631,500	147,280,000	182,514,300
Eastern Orthodox	4,189,000	552,000	50,545,000
Protestant	95,279,200	11,148,000	115,000,000
Jewish	6,641,118	727,000	4,082,400
Muslim	249,200	238,300	8,283,500
Zoroastrian	250	2,000	6,000
Shinto	60,000	92,000	—
Taoist	16,000	12,000	—
Confucian	96,100	85,150	25,000
Buddhist	155,250	195,300	200,000
Hindu	81,000	782,300	260,000
Totals	238,398,618	161,114,050	360,916,200
Population	353,560,000	230,139,000	738,746,000

A few observations

One fourth of the world population professes the Christian faith. *Three fourths* of the world population profess other faiths or adhere to a secular conviction. And given the geographical spread of that division, it is likely that by the year 2000, less than *one fifth* of the world population will be Christian.

The World Council of Churches' membership groups together about 400 million Christians. The Roman Catholic Church has over 150 million more members than all the other Christian churches together. Africa and Oceania are the only continents where Roman Catholics do not outnumber both Eastern Orthodox and Protestants together.

Both the Muslim and Hindu world community have more faithful than all the Orthodox and Protestant churches which belong to the World Council of Churches. The Muslim population of Africa, for instance, is as large as the continent's entire Christian population.

Asia	Africa	Oceania	World
89,909,000	137,460,300	18,112,600	983,620,900
47,046,000	53,740,000	4,475,000	566,686,800
1,894,000	15,255,000	380,000	72,815,000
40,969,000	68,465,300	13,257,600	344,119,100
3,203,460	294,400	84,000	15,032,378
433,001,000	134,285,200	103,000	576,160,200
224,700	600	—	233,550
55,004,000	—	—	55,156,000
31,088,100	—	—	31,116,100
173,940,250	500	42,200	174,189,200
260,117,000	2,000	16,000	260,685,550
515,449,500	483,650	841,000	517,897,450
1,561,937,010	272,526,650	19,198,800	2,614,091,328
2,355,700,000	423,655,000	22,157,000	4,123,957,000

Buddhism has several modern renewal movements which have gained adherents in Europe and America and other areas that do not have an ethnic tradition of Buddhism. Hinduism's strength in India has been enhanced by nationalism, although modern Hinduism has also developed renewal movements that have made converts in Europe and America.

Almost half of the Jewish world population lives in North America. Only one fifth of all Jews are citizens of Israel.

Almost 35% of the world's population do not profess a religious faith but either adhere to a secular ideology or profess no convictions at all. Where ideological regimes have been established which are opposed to all "religion", as in most countries under Communist control, it is difficult to obtain reliable information on the continuing strength of the older world views.

The statistics, which are all estimates, are taken from the *Britannica Book of the Year 1978*.

62

APPENDIX II
MILESTONES IN THE ECUMENICAL MOVEMENT

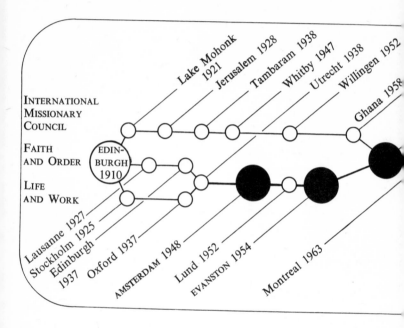

APPENDIX III
MEMBERSHIP IN THE WORLD COUNCIL

Amsterdam, 1948	146 churches
Evanston, 1954	163 churches
New Delhi, 1961	198 churches
Uppsala, 1968	235 churches
Nairobi, 1975	286 churches

Present total membership: 293 churches

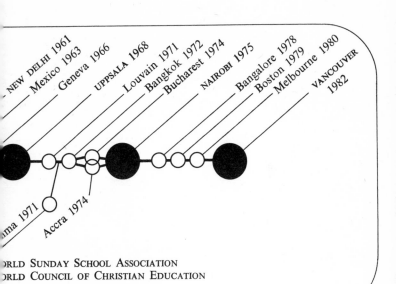

NEW DELHI 1961
Mexico 1963
Geneva 1966
UPPSALA 1968
Louvain 1971
Bangkok 1972
Bucharest 1974
NAIROBI 1975
Bangalore 1978
Boston 1979
Melbourne 1980
VANCOUVER 1982

ama 1971
Accra 1974

ORLD SUNDAY SCHOOL ASSOCIATION
ORLD COUNCIL OF CHRISTIAN EDUCATION

APPENDIX IV
CENTRAL COMMITTEE MEETINGS

1948	Woudschoten	1957	New Haven	1968	Uppsala
1949	Chichester	1958	Nyborg Strand	1969	Canterbury
1950	Toronto	1959	Rhodes	1971	Addis Ababa
1951	Rolle	1960	St Andrews	1972	Utrecht
1952-3	Lucknow	1961	New Delhi	1973	Geneva
1954	Chicago	1962	Paris	1974	Berlin (West)
1954	Evanston	1963	Rochester	1975	Nairobi
1955	Davos	1965	Enugu	1976	Geneva
1956	Galyatetö	1966	Geneva	1977	Geneva
		1967	Heraklion	1979	Kingston

APPENDIX V
ORGANIZATIONAL CHART OF THE WCC

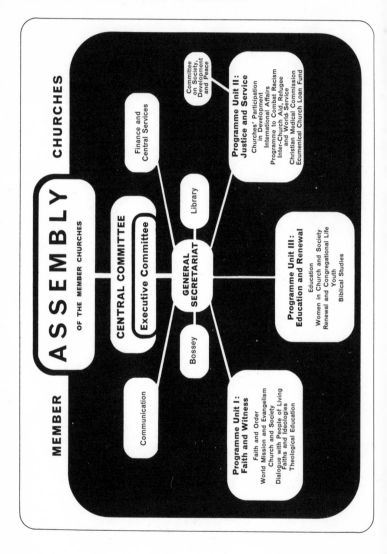

APPENDIX VI
PRESIDENTS AND EXECUTIVE OFFICERS OF THE WCC

Presidents

Dr W. A. Visser 't Hooft, Honorary President, Switzerland

Mrs Justice Annie Jiagge, Ghana

Dr José Miguez Bonino, Argentina

Metropolitan Nikodim, USSR

Dr T. B. Simatupang, Indonesia

Archbishop Olof Sundby, Sweden

Dr Cynthia Wedel, USA

Executive Officers

Archbishop Edward Scott, Canada (Moderator)

Ms Jean Skuse, Australia, and Coadjutor Catholicos Karekin II, USA
(Vice Moderators)

Rev. Dr Philip A. Potter, Dominica (General Secretary of the WCC)

APPENDIX VII
STAFF OF THE WORLD COUNCIL

	Executive Staff	Secretarial and Administrative Staff	Total
Africa	7	4	11
Asia	10	2	12
Australasia	3	2	5
Latin America and the Caribbean	9	5	14
North America	16	3	19
Eastern Europe	2	1	3
Western Europe	61	150	211
Total	108	167	275

APPENDIX VIII
THE WCC BUDGET

Each year the equivalent of approximately US $50 million flows through the books of the Council, including some US $35 million en route to victims of human and man-made disasters, and to finance everything from leadership training scholarships to evangelistic activities to rural development schemes.

The churches and their agencies provide nearly 95% of the total cash flow of the World Council. The remaining money for particular projects comes from secular and governmental organizations, and foundations.

US $15 million pays for the World Council's own operations and programmes, and is divided up in the following way:

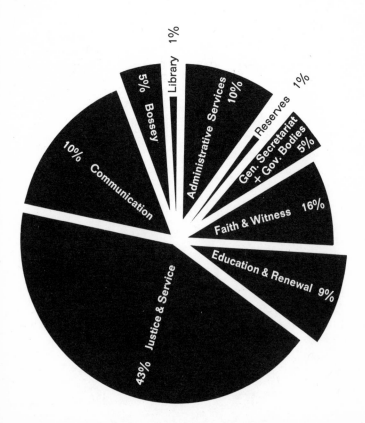

The budget for each of the three units is divided up as follows:

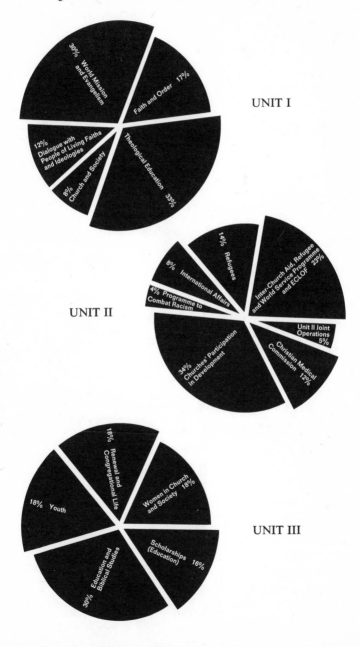

UNIT I

30% World Mission and Evangelism
17% Faith and Order
33% Theological Education
8% Church and Society
12% Dialogue with People of Living Faiths and Ideologies

UNIT II

14% Refugees
8% International Affairs
4% Programme to Combat Racism
23% Inter-Church Aid, Refugee and World Service Programme and ECLOF
5% Unit II Joint Operations
12% Christian Medical Commission
34% Churches' Participation in Development

UNIT III

18% Renewal and Congregational Life
18% Women in Church and Society
18% Youth
16% Scholarships (Education)
30% Education and Biblical Studies

APPENDIX IX

MEMBER CHURCHES, ASSOCIATE MEMBER CHURCHES AND ASSOCIATE COUNCILS OF THE WCC

* Associate member church

ALGERIA

Eglise Protestante d'Algérie *
(Protestant Church of Algeria)

ARGENTINA

Iglesia Evangélica Luterana Unida *
(United Evangelical Lutheran Church)

Iglesia Evangélica Metodista Argentina
(Evangelical Methodist Church of Argentina)

Iglesia Evangélica del Río de la Plata
(Evangelical Church of the River Plata)

Junta de los Discipulos de Cristo *
(Disciples of Christ)

AUSTRALIA

Australian Council of Churches

Churches of Christ in Australia

The Church of England in Australia

The Presbyterian Church of Australia

The Uniting Church in Australia

AUSTRIA

Alt-katholische Kirche Österreichs
(Old Catholic Church of Austria)

Evangelische Kirche Augsburgischen u. Helvetischen Bekenntnisses (A.u.H.B.)
(Evangelical Church of the Augsburg and Helvetic Confession)

Ökumenischer Rat der Kirchen in Österreich
(Ecumenical Council of Austrian Churches)

BANGLADESH

Bangladesh Baptist Sangha

The Church of Bangladesh *

BELGIUM

Eglise Protestante de Belgique
(Protestant Church of Belgium)

Eglise Réformée de Belgique
(Reformed Church of Belgium)

BOLIVIA

Iglesia Evangélica Metodista en Bolivia *
(Evangelical Methodist Church in Bolivia)

BOTSWANA

Christian Council of Botswana

BRAZIL

Igreja Episcopal do Brasil
(Episcopal Church of Brazil)

Igreja Evangélica de Confissão Lutherana do Brasil
(Evangelical Church of Lutheran Confession in Brazil)

Igreja Evangélica Pentecostal "O Brasil para Cristo"
(The Evangelical Pentecostal Church "Brazil for Christ")

Igreja Metodista do Brasil
(Methodist Church of Brazil)

Igreja Reformada Latino Americana
(The Latin American Reformed Church)

BULGARIA

Eglise Orthodoxe Bulgare
(Bulgarian Orthodox Church)

BURMA

Burma Baptist Convention

Burma Council of Churches

Church of the Province of Burma

CAMEROON

Eglise évangélique du Cameroun
(Evangelical Church of Cameroon)

Eglise presbytérienne camérou-
naise
(Presbyterian Church of
Cameroon)

Eglise Protestante Africaine *
(African Protestant Church)

Presbyterian Church in Cameroon

Union des Eglises baptistes du
Cameroun
(Union of Baptist Churches of
Cameroon)

CANADA

The Anglican Church of Canada

Canadian Council of Churches

Canadian Yearly Meeting of the
Society of Friends

Christian Church (Disciples of
Christ)

The Evangelical Lutheran Church
of Canada

The Presbyterian Church in
Canada

The United Church of Canada

CENTRAL AFRICA

Church of the Province of Central
Africa

CHILE

Iglesia Evangélica Luterana en
Chile
(Evangelical-Lutheran Church in
Chile)

Iglesia Metodista de Chile *
(The Methodist Church of Chile)

Iglesia Pentecostal de Chile
(Pentecostal Church of Chile)

Misión Iglesia Pentecostal
(Pentecostal Mission Church)

CHINA

China Baptist Council

Chung-Hua Chi-Tu Chiao-Hui
(Church of Christ in China)

Chung Hua Sheng Kung Hui
(Anglican Church in China)

Hua Pei Kung Lu Hui
(North China Union of
Congregational Churches)

CONGO (People's Republic of the)

Eglise Evangélique du Congo
(Evangelical Church of the
Congo)

COOK ISLANDS

Cook Islands Christian Church

COSTA RICA

Iglesia Evangélica Metodista de
Costa Rica *
(Evangelical Methodist Church of
Costa Rica)

CUBA

Iglesia Metodista en Cuba *
(Methodist Church in Cuba)

Iglesia Presbiteriana-Reformada
en Cuba *
(Presbyterian-Reformed Church
in Cuba)

CYPRUS

Church of Cyprus

CZECHOSLOVAKIA

Českobratrská církev evangelická
(Evangelical Church of Czech
Brethren)

Československá církev husitská
(Czechoslovak Hussite Church)

Ecumenical Council of Churches
in the Czech Socialist Republic

Pravoslavná církev v ČSSR
(Orthodox Church of Czechoslo-
vakia)

Ref. krest. církev na Slovensku
(Reformed Christian Church in
Slovakia)

Slezská církev evangelická a.v.
(Silesian Evangelical Church of
the Augsburg Confession)

Slovenská evanjelická církev a.v.
v. ČSSR
(Slovak Evangelical Church of the
Augsb. Conf. in the CSSR)

BENIN (DAHOMEY)

Eglise Protestante Méthodiste au
Bénin-Togo
(The Protestant Methodist Church
in Bénin-Togo)

DENMARK

Det danske Baptistsamfund
(The Baptist Union of Denmark)

Ecumenical Council of Denmark

Den evangelisk-lutherske Folke-
kirke i Danmark
(The Church of Denmark)

EAST AFRICA

Presbyterian Church of East
Africa

EGYPT

Coptic Orthodox Church

Evangelical Church — The Synod
of the Nile

Greek Orthodox Patriarchate of
Alexandria

EQUATORIAL GUINEA

Iglesia Evangélica de Guinea
Ecuatorial *
(Evangelical Church of Equatorial
Guinea)

ETHIOPIA

Ethiopia Orthodox Church

FIJI

Methodist Church in Fiji

FINLAND

Ecumenical Council of Finland

Suomen Evankelis-Luterilainen
Kirkko
(Evangelical-Lutheran Church
of Finland)

FRANCE

Eglise de la Confession d'Augs-
bourg d'Alsace et de Lorraine
(Evangelical Church of the Augsburg Confession of Alsace and
Lorraine)

Eglise Evangélique Luthérienne
de France
(Evangelical Lutheran Church of
France)

Eglise Réformée d'Alsace et de
Lorraine
(Reformed Church of Alsace and
Lorraine)

Eglise Réformée de France
(Reformed Church of France)

GABONESE REPUBLIC

Eglise Evangélique du Gabon
(Evangelical Church of Gabon)

**FEDERAL REPUBLIC OF
GERMANY**

Arbeitsgemeinschaft Christlicher
Kirchen in Deutschland
(Council of Christian Churches in
Germany (FRG))

Evangelische Brüder-Unität
(Moravian Church)

Evangelische Kirche in Deutschland
(Evangelical Church in Germany)

  Evangelische Landeskirche in
  Baden

  Evangelisch-Lutherische
  Kirche in Bayern **

** This Church is directly a
member of the World Council of
Churches in accordance with the
resolution of the General Synod of
the United Evangelical Lutheran
Church of Germany, dated 27 Jan-
uary 1949, which recommended
that the member churches of the
United Evangelical Lutheran Church
should make the following declar-
ation to the Council of the Evangelical Church in Germany concerning their relation to the World
Council of Churches:
"The Evangelical Church in Germany has made it clear through its
constitution that it is a federation
(Bund) of confessionally determined
churches. Moreover, the condi-
tions of membership of the World
Council of Churches have been
determined at the Assembly at
Amsterdam. Therefore, this Evangelical Lutheran Church declares
concerning its membership in the
World Council of Churches:
(i) It is represented in the World
Council as a church of the
Evangelical Lutheran confession.
(ii) Representatives which it sends
to the World Council are to be
identified as Evangelical Lutherans.
(iii) Within the limits of the
competence of the Evangelical
Church in Germany it is represented in the World Council
through the intermediary of the
Evangelical Church in Germany."

Evangelische Kirche in Berlin-Brandenburg

Evangelisch-Lutherische Landeskirche in Braunschweig **

Bremische Evangelische Kirche

Evangelisch-Lutherische Landeskirche Hannovers **

Evangelische Kirche in Hessen und Nassau

Evangelische Kirche von Kurhessen-Waldeck

Lippische Landeskirche

Nordelbische Evangelisch-Lutherische Kirche **

Evangelisch-Reformierte Kirche in Nordwestdeutschland

Evangelisch-Lutherische Kirche in Oldenburg

Vereinigte Protestantisch-Evangelisch-Christliche Kirche der Pfalz

Evangelische Kirche im Rheinland

Evangelisch-Lutherische Landeskirche Schaumburg-Lippe **

Evangelische Kirche von Westfalen

Evangelische Landeskirche in Württemberg

Katholisches Bistum der Alt-Katholiken in Deutschland
(Catholic Diocese of the Old Catholics in Germany)

Vereinigung der Deutschen Mennonitengemeinden
(Mennonite Church)

GERMAN DEMOCRATIC REPUBLIC

Arbeitsgemeinschaft Christlicher Kirchen in der DDR
(Council of Christian Churches (GDR)

Bund der Evangelischen Kirchen in der Deutschen Demokratischen Republik

(Federation of the Evangelical Churches in the GDR)

Evangelische Landeskirche Anhalts ***

Evangelische Kirche in Berlin-Brandenburg ***

Evangelische Kirche des Görlitzer Kirchengebietes ***

Evangelische Landeskirche Greifswald ***

Evangelisch-Lutherische Landeskirche Mecklenburgs ***

Evangelische Kirche der Kirchenprovinz Sachsen ***

Evangelisch-Lutherische Landeskirche Sachsens ***

Evangelisch-Lutherische Kirche in Thüringen ***

Evangelische Brüder-Unität (Distrikt Herrnhut)
(Moravian Church)

Gemeindeverband der Alt-Katholischen Kirche in der Deutschen Demokratischen Republik
(Federation of the Old Catholic Church in the GDR)

GHANA

The Christian Council of Ghana

Evangelical Presbyterian Church

The Methodist Church, Ghana

Presbyterian Church of Ghana

GREECE

Ekklesia tes Ellados
(Church of Greece)

Hellenike Evangelike Ekklesia
(Greek Evangelical Church)

HONG KONG

The Church of Christ in China, The Hong Kong Council

Hong Kong Christian Council

*** United in a fellowship of Christian witness and service in the Federation of Evangelical Churches in the GDR, these churches are represented in the Council through agencies of the Federation of Evangelical Churches in the GDR.

** See note p. 70.

HUNGARY

Ecumenical Council in Hungary

Magyarországi Baptista Egyház
(Baptist Church in Hungary)

Magyarországi Evangélikus
Egyház
(Lutheran Church in Hungary)

Magyarországi Református
Egyház
(Reformed Church in Hungary)

ICELAND

Evangelical Lutheran Church of
Iceland

INDIA

Bengal-Orissa-Bihar Baptist
Convention *

Church of North India

Church of South India

Mar Thoma Syrian Church of
Malabar

National Christian Council of
India

The Orthodox Syrian Church,
Catholicate of the East

The Samavesam of Telugu
Baptist Churches

United Evangelical Lutheran
Churches in India

INDONESIA

Banua Niha Keriso Protestan
Nias
(The Church of Nias)

Christian Protestant Church in
Indonesia

Council of Churches in Indonesia

Gereja Batak Karo Protestan
(Karo Batak Protestant Church)

Gereja-Gereja Kristen Java
(Christian Churches of Java)

Gereja Kalimantan Evangelis
(Kalimantan Evangelical Church)

Gereja Kristen Indonesia
(Indonesian Christian Church)

Gereja Kristen Injili di Irian Jaya
(Evangelical Christian Church in
West Irian)

Gereja Kristen Jawi Wetan
(Christian Church of East Java)

Gereja Kristen Pasundan
(Pasundan Christian Church)

Gereja Kristen Protestan Di Bali *
(Protestant Christian Church in
Bali)

Gereja Kristen Protestan
Simalungun
(Simalungun Protestant Christian
Church)

Gereja Kristen Sulawesi Tengah
(Christian Church in Mid-
Sulawesi)

Gereja Masehi Injili Minahasa
(Christian Evangelical Church in
Minahasa)

Gereja Masehi Injili Sangihe
Talaud (GMIST)
(Evangelical Church of Sangir
Talaud)

Gereja Masehi Injili di Timor
(Protestant Evangelical Church
in Timor)

Gereja Protestan di Indonesia
(Protestant Church in Indonesia)

Gereja Protestan Maluku
(Protestant Church of the
Moluccas)

Gereja Toraja
(Toraja Church)

Huria Kristen Batak Protestan
(Protestant Christian Batak
Church)

Huria Kristen Indonesia (H.K.I.)
(The Indonesian Christian
Church)

Punguan Kristen Batak (P.K.B.) *

IRAN

Apostolic Catholic Assyrian
Church of the East

Synod of the Evangelical Church
of Iran

ITALY

Chiesa Evangelica Metodista
d'Italia
(Evangelical Methodist Church of
Italy)

Chiesa Evangelica Valdese
(Waldensian Church)

Evangelical Baptist Union of
Italy *

JAMAICA

The Moravian Church in Jamaica

The United Church of Jamaica
and Grand Cayman

JAPAN

Japanese Orthodox Church

The Korean Christian Church in
Japan *

The National Christian Council
of Japan

Nippon Kirisuto Kyodan
(The United Church of Christ in
Japan)

Nippon Sei Ko Kai
(Anglican-Episcopal Church in
Japan)

JERUSALEM

Episcopal Church in Jerusalem
and the Middle East

Greek Orthodox Patriarchate of
Jerusalem

KENYA

African Christian Church and
Schools

African Church of the Holy
Spirit *

African Israel Church, Nineveh

Church of the Province of Kenya

The Methodist Church in Kenya

KOREA

The Korean Methodist Church

The Presbyterian Church in the
Republic of Korea

The Presbyterian Church of Korea

LEBANON

Armenian Apostolic Church

Union of the Armenian Evangelical Churches in the Near East

LESOTHO

Lesotho Evangelical Church

LIBERIA

Lutheran Church in Liberia

Presbytery of Liberia *

MADAGASCAR

Eglise de Jésus-Christ à Mada-
gascar
(Church of Jesus Christ in Mada-
gascar)

Eglise Luthérienne Malgache
(Malagasy Lutheran Church)

MALAYSIA

Council of Churches in Malaysia

The Methodist Church in
Malaysia

Protestant Church in Sabah *

MAURITIUS

Church of the Province of the
Indian Ocean

MEXICO

Iglesia Metodista de México
(Methodist Church of Mexico)

NETHERLANDS

Algemene Doopsgezinde Sociëteit
(General Mennonite Society)

Council of Churches in the
Netherlands

Evangelisch Lutherse Kerk
(Evangelical Lutheran Church)

De Gereformeerde Kerken in
Nederland
(The Reformed Churches in the
Netherlands)

Nederlandse Hervormde Kerk
(Netherlands Reformed Church)

Oud-Katholieke Kerk van
Nederland
(Old Catholic Church of the
Netherlands)

Remonstrantse Broederschap
(Remonstrant Brotherhood)

NETHERLANDS ANTILLES

Iglesia Protestant Uni *
(United Protestant Church)

NEW CALEDONIA

Eglise Evangélique en Nouvelle-Calédonie et aux Iles Loyauté
(Evangelical Church in New Caledonia and the Loyalty Isles)

NEW HEBRIDES

Presbyterian Church of the New Hebrides

NEW ZEALAND

Associated Churches of Christ in New Zealand

The Baptist Union of New Zealand

Church of the Province of New Zealand

The Methodist Church of New Zealand

National Council of Churches in New Zealand

The Presbyterian Church of New Zealand

NIGERIA

The Church of the Lord Aladura

Methodist Church, Nigeria

Nigerian Baptist Convention

The Presbyterian Church of Nigeria

NORWAY

Den Norske Kirke
(Church of Norway)

PAKISTAN

The Church of Pakistan

United Presbyterian Church of Pakistan

PAPUA NEW GUINEA

The United Church in Papua, New Guinea and the Solomon Islands

PERU

Iglesia Metodista del Peru *

PHILIPPINES

Iglesia Evangélica Metodista en las Islas Filipinas
(The Evangelical Methodist Church in the Philippines)

Iglesia Filipina Independiente
(Philippine Independent Church)

National Council of Churches in the Philippines

United Church of Christ in the Philippines

POLAND

Autocephalic Orthodox Church in Poland

Kosciola Ewangelicko-Augsburskiego w PRL
(Evangelical Church of the Augsburg Confession in Poland)

Kosciola Polskokatolickiego w PRL
(Polish Catholic Church in Poland)

Polish Ecumenical Council

Staro-Katolickiego Kosciola Mariatowitow w PRL
(Old Catholic Mariavite Church in Poland)

PORTUGAL

Igreja Evangélica Presbiteriana de Portugal *
(Evangelical Presbyterian Church of Portugal)

Igreja Lusitana Catolica Apostolica Evangélica *
(Lusitanian Catholic-Apostolic Evangelical Church)

RHODESIA

Christian Council of Rhodesia

ROMANIA

Biserica Evangelică După Confesiunea Dela Augsburg
(Evangelical Church of the Augsburg Confession)

Biserica Ortodoxă Române
(Romanian Orthodox Church)

Biserica Reformată Din Romania
(Reformed Church of Romania)

Evangelical Synodal Presbyterial Church of the Augsburg Confession in the Socialist Republic of Romania

SAMOA

The Congregational Christian Church in Samoa

Methodist Church of Samoa *

SIERRA LEONE

The Methodist Church Sierra Leone

SINGAPORE

The Methodist Church in Singapore *

National Council of Churches of Singapore

SOLOMON ISLANDS

Church of Melanesia

SOUTH AFRICA

The Bantu Presbyterian Church of South Africa

Church of the Province of South Africa

Evangelical Lutheran Church in Southern Africa

The Methodist Church of South Africa

Moravian Church in South Africa

The Presbyterian Church of Southern Africa

The South African Council of Churches

The United Congregational Church of Southern Africa

SPAIN

Iglesia Española Reformada Episcopal *
(Spanish Reformed Episcopal Church)

Iglesia Evangélica Española
(Spanish Evangelical Church)

SRI LANKA

The Church of Ceylon

Methodist Church

National Christian Council of Sri Lanka

SUDAN

Episcopal Church of the Sudan

The Presbyterian Church in the Sudan *

SURINAM

Moravian Church in Surinam

SWEDEN

Svenska Kyrkan
(Church of Sweden)

Svenska Missionsförbundet

Swedish Ecumenical Council

SWITZERLAND

Christkatholische Kirche der Schweiz
(Old Catholic Church of Switzerland)

Schweizerischer Evangelischer Kirchenbund
Fédération des Eglises protestantes de la Suisse
(Swiss Protestant Church Federation)

SYRIA

The National Evangelical Synod of Syria and Lebanon

Patriarcat Grec-Orthodoxe d'Antioche et de tout l'Orient
(Greek Orthodox Patriarchate of Antioch and All the East)

Syrian Orthodox Patriarchate of Antioch and All the East

TAHITI

Eglise évangélique de Polynésie française
(Evangelical Church of French Polynesia)

TANZANIA

Church of the Province of Tanzania

Evangelical Lutheran Church in Tanzania

THAILAND

The Church of Christ in Thailand

TOGO

Eglise évangélique du Togo
(Evangelical Church of Togo)

TONGA

Free Wesleyan Church of Tonga

TRINIDAD

The Presbyterian Church in
Trinidad and Grenada

TURKEY

Ecumenical Patriarchate of
Constantinople

UGANDA

The Church of Uganda, Rwanda
and Burundi

**UNION OF SOVIET
SOCIALIST REPUBLICS**

Eesti Evangeeliumi Luteri usu
Kirik
(Estonian Evangelical Lutheran
Church)

Eglise apostolique arménienne
(Armenian Apostolic Church)

Georgian Orthodox Church,
David V

Latvijas Evangeliska-Luteriska
Baznica
(Evangelical Lutheran Church of
Latvia)

Russian Orthodox Church

The Union of Evangelical
Christian Baptists of USSR

**UNITED KINGDOM AND
REPUBLIC OF IRELAND**

British Council of Churches

England

The Baptist Union of Great
Britain and Ireland

Churches of Christ in Great
Britain and Ireland

The Church of England

The Methodist Church

The Moravian Union

The Salvation Army

The United Reformed Church in
England and Wales

Ireland

The Church of Ireland

The Methodist Church in Ireland

The Presbyterian Church in
Ireland

Scotland

The Church of Scotland

The Congregational Union of
Scotland

Episcopal Church in Scotland

United Free Church of Scotland

Wales

The Church in Wales

The Presbyterian Church of
Wales

Union of Welsh Independents

**UNITED STATES OF
AMERICA**

African Methodist Episcopal
Church

African Methodist Episcopal Zion
Church

American Baptist Churches in the
U.S.A.

American Lutheran Church

The Antiochian Orthodox
Christian Archdiocese of New
York and all North America

Christian Church (Disciples of
Christ)

Christian Methodist Episcopal
Church

Church of the Brethren

The Episcopal Church

Hungarian Reformed Church in
America

International Evangelical Church

Lutheran Church in America

Moravian Church in America
(Northern Province)

Moravian Church in America
(Southern Province)

National Baptist Convention of
America

National Baptist Convention,
U.S.A., Inc.

National Council of the Churches
of Christ in the U.S.A.

National Council of Community
Churches

The Orthodox Church in
America

Polish National Catholic Church
of America

Presbyterian Church in the United
States

Progressive National Baptist
Convention

Reformed Church in America

Religious Society of Friends
Friends General Conference
Friends United Meeting

United Church of Christ

The United Methodist Church

The United Presbyterian Church
in the United States of America

URUGUAY

Iglesia Evangélica Metodista en el
Uruguay *
(The Evangelical Methodist
Church in Uruguay)

WEST AFRICA

The Church of the Province of
West Africa

WEST INDIES

The Church in the Province of the
West Indies

The Methodist Church in the
Caribbean and the Americas

Moravian Church, Eastern West
Indies Province

YUGOSLAVIA

Ecumenical Council of Churches
in Yugoslavia

Reformatska Crke u SFRJ
(The Reformed Church in
Yugoslavia)

Serbian Orthodox Church

Slovenska ev.-kr. a.v. cirkev v.
Juhuslavii
(Slovak Evangelical Church of the
Augsburg Confession in
Yugoslavia)

ZAÏRE (Republic of)

Eglise du Christ au Zaïre (Com-
munauté des Disciples)
(Church of Christ in Zaïre —
Community of Disciples)

Eglise du Christ au Zaïre
(52 Communauté Lumière)
(Church of Christ in Zaïre —
Community the Light)

Eglise du Christ au Zaïre (Com-
munauté Mennonite au Zaïre)
(Church of Christ in Zaïre —
Mennonite Community in
Zaïre)

Eglise du Christ au Zaïre (Com-
munauté épiscopale baptiste en
Afrique C.E.B.A.) *
(Church of Christ in Zaïre)

Eglise du Christ sur la Terre par
le Prophète Simon Kimbangu
(Church of Christ on Earth by the
Prophet Simon Kimbangu)

Eglise évangélique du Zaïre
(Evangelical Church of Zaïre)

Eglise presbytérienne au Zaïre
(Presbyterian Church in Zaïre)

ZAMBIA

United Church of Zambia

OTHER CHURCHES

Eesti Evangeeliumi Luteri Usu
Kirik
(Estonian Evangelical Lutheran
Church)

Latvijas Evangeliska Luteriska
Baznica
(Latvian Evangelical Lutheran
Church) (In Exile)

APPENDIX X

MEMBERS OF THE CENTRAL COMMITTEE

*Executive Committee member

Most Rev. S.H. Ajamian
Armenian Apostolic Church

Rt Rev. John M. Allin
Episcopal Church, USA

Bishop Ralph T. Alton
United Methodist Church, USA

Mr Jan Anchimiuk
Autocephalic Orthodox Church
in Poland

Mrs Joan Anderson
Presbyterian Church
of New Zealand

Dr Rakoto-Andrianarijaona
Malagasy Lutheran Church

*Rev. Dr André Appel
Evangelical Church of the
Augsburg Confession of Alsace
and Lorraine, France

Mr Harry A. Ashmall
Church of Scotland

*Prof. Dr Anwar M. Barkat
Church of Pakistan

Bishop Dr Tibor Bartha
Reformed Church in Hungary

*Mr Bena-Silu
Church of Christ on Earth, Zaïre

Rt Rev. Dr P. A. Berberian
Armenian Apostolic Church

Rev. Alexei Bichkov
Union of Evangelical Christian
Baptists of USSR

Rev. Jacques Blanc
Protestant Church of Algeria

Rev. Prof. Vitaly Borovoy
Russian Orthodox Church

Rev. Leslie Boseto
United Church in Papua-New
Guinea and the Solomon Islands

Hon. Mr John Brademas
United Methodist Church, USA

Dr Arie R. Brouwer
Reformed Church in America

Rev. John P. Brown
Presbyterian Church of Australia

Rt Rev. J. L. Bryce
Church of the Province
of New Zealand

Mr Alexey Buevsky
Russian Orthodox Church

Dr Robert Campbell
American Baptist Churches
in the USA

Rev. Chan Chor Choi
Anglican Church of China
including Hong Kong

*His Eminence Konstantinidis
Chrysostomos
Ecumenical Patriarchate

Metropolitan Parthenios-Aris
Coinidis, Greek Orthodox
Patriarchate of Alexandria

Mrs Fernanda Comba
Waldensian Church, Italy

Rev. Dr Paul Crow, Jr
Christian Church
(Disciples of Christ), USA

Rev. E. A. Dahunsi
Nigerian Baptist Convention

Rev. Meirion Lloyd Davies
Presbyterian Church of Wales,
UK

Mr John Doom
Evangelical Church
of French Polynesia

Rev. Canon E.P.M. Elliott
Church of Ireland

Principal Olle Engstrom
Mission Covenant Church
of Sweden

Prof. Dr Hans Helmut Esser
Evangelical Church in Germany
(Reformed), FRG

Miss Ana B. Ferrari
Evangelical Methodist Church
of Argentina

Mr Ludwig Franke
Evangelical Lutheran Church
of Thuringia, GDR

Dr Hans Alfred Frei
Old Catholic Church
of Switzerland

*Rev. John G. Gatu
Presbyterian Church
of East Africa

Mrs Daisy Gopal Ratnam
Church of South India

Rev. David X. J. Gqweta
Moravian Church
in South Africa

*Metropolitan Paulos Gregorios
Orthodox Syrian Church
Catholicate of the East

Rev. Dr John S. Groenfeldt
Moravian Church in America
(Northern Province)

Prof. Dr Gerhard Grohs
Evangelical Church in Germany
United, FRG

*Bishop Hans Heinrich Harms
Evangelical Church in Germany
Lutheran, FRG

Metropolitan Ignatios Hazim
Greek Orthodox Patriarchate
of Antioch and All the East

Dr Heinz Joachim Held
Evangelical Church in Germany
Lutheran, FRG

*Bishop Dr Johannes Wilhelm
Hempel, Evangelical Church
of Saxony, GDR

Rev. Harry Henry
Protestant Methodist Church
in Dahomey and Togo

Rev. Dr Albert van den Heuvel
Netherlands Reformed Church

Bishop Dr Friedrich Huebner
Evangelical Church in Germany
Lutheran, FRG

Rev. Albert Isteero
Evangelical Church
Synod of the Nile

His Grace Zakka Iwas
Syrian Orthodox Patriarchate
of Antioch and All the East

Dr Joseph H. Jackson
National Baptist Convention
USA Inc.

Dr Emil A. Jeevaratnam
Methodist Church, Sri Lanka

Mrs Heather Johnston
Presbyterian Church in Canada

Bishop Frederick D. Jordan
African Methodist Episcopal
Church, USA

His Eminence Juvenaly
of Tula and Belev
Russian Orthodox Church

*Rev. Dr Won Yong Kang
Presbyterian Church
in the Republic of Korea

Rt Rev. Dr Josiah M. Kibira
Evangelical Lutheran Church
in Tanzania

*Very Rev. Kirill (Gundyayev)
Russian Orthodox Church

Bishop Chester A. Kirkendoll
Christian Methodist Episcopal
Church, USA

Bishop Albert Klein
Evangelical Church of the
Augsburg Confession, Romania

Prof. Gerasimos Konidaris
Church of Greece

Most Rev. Arthur Kratz
Episcopal Church of Brazil

Ms Julia Lädrach
Swiss Protestant Church
Federation

Rev. Johannes Langhoff
Church of Denmark

Miss Cynthia Latuihamallo
Protestant Church in Indonesia

Rev. Samuel Lehtonen
Evangelical Lutheran Church
of Finland

Mr José Leite
Evangelical Presbyterian
Church of Portugal

Rt Rev. Per Lønning
Church of Norway

Ms Janice Love
United Methodist Church, USA

Rev. Augustina Lumentut
Christian Church
in Mid-Sulawesi, Indonesia

Rev. Wilson T. Lwanga-
Mugerwa
Church of Uganda, Rwanda
Burundi and Boga Zaire

Miss Evelyn Mahlatsi
Church of the Province
of South Africa

Mr Renato Z. Malvar
Philippine Independent Church

*Rev. Dr Robert J. Marshall
Lutheran Church in America

Bishop James K. Mathews
United Methodist Church, USA

Miss Teli Matthew
Federation of Evangelical
Lutheran Churches in India

Archbishop Janis Matulis
Evangelical Lutheran Church
of Latvia

Mrs Jean Mayland
Church of England

*Rev. J. Oscar McCloud
United Presbyterian Church
in the USA

Pastor Manoel de Mello
Evangelical Pentecostal Church
"Brazil for Christ"

Rev. Prof. Jean Meyendorff
Orthodox Church in America

Mrs Marie Momo Kingue
Evangelical Church of Cameroon

Rev. Armencius Munthe
Simalungun Protestant
Christian Church, Indonesia

Rt Rev. Gerald B. Muston
Church of England in Australia

Dr Emerito P. Nacpil
United Methodist Church
Philippines

His Eminence Nicolas
Romanian Orthodox Church

Prof. Dr Nikos A. Nissiotis
Church of Greece

Rev. Francisco Norniella
Presbyterian Reformed Church
in Cuba

Pastor Lukombo-Kitete
Ntontolo, Evangelical Church
of Zaïre

Dr Maurice Nyembezi
Methodist Church
of South Africa

Ms Mercy Oduyoye
Methodist Church, Nigeria

Rt Rev. Dr Henry Okullu
Church of the Province of Kenya

Metropolitan Pankratij
Bulgarian Orthodox Church

Metropolitan Paul
(Menevichoglou) of Sweden
Ecumenical Patriarchate
of Constantinople

Bishop Paulos
Ethiopian Orthodox Church

Rev. Margaret Barnes Peery
Presbyterian Church
in the United States

Miss Waltraut Peper
Evangelical Church of Anhalt
GDR

*Rt Rev. Antonie Plamadeala
Romanian Orthodox Church

Rev. Dr Avery Post
United Church of Christ, USA

Mr Albert J. Price
United Church of Christ, USA

Prof. Warren Quanbeck
American Lutheran Church

Deacon Radomir Rakic
Serbian Orthodox Church

*Dr Jacques Rossel
Swiss Protestant Church
Federation

Rev. Dr David S. Russell
Baptist Union of Great Britain
and Ireland

*Mrs Dorinda Sampath
Presbyterian Church
in Trinidad and Grenada

His Grace Bishop Samuel
Coptic Orthodox Church, Egypt

*His Holiness Karekin II
Armenian Apostolic Church
(*Vice-Moderator*)

*Most Rev. Edward W. Scott
Anglican Church of Canada
(*Moderator*)

Rt Rev. Gurbachan Singh
Church of North India

*Ms Jean Skuse
Methodist Church in Australia
(*Vice-Moderator*)

Prof. Josef Smolik
Evangelical Church
of Czech Brethren

Rt Rev. Neville W. de Souza
Church in the Province
of the West Indies

Dr Koson Srisang
Church of Christ in Thailand

Rev. Dr Sutarno
Christian Churches of Java

Mr Nikolay Teteryatnikov
Russian Orthodox Church

Prof. Kyaw Than
Burma Baptist Convention

Dr M. M. Thomas
Mar Thoma Syrian Church
of Malabar, India

Ms Barbara R. Thompson
United Methodist Church, USA

Mr William P. Thompson
United Presbyterian Church
in the USA

Mr Habte Tsegaye
Ethiopian Orthodox Church

Mrs Marja van der Veen-
Schenkeveld, Reformed
Churches in the Netherlands

Rev. Dr Robert A. Wallace
United Church of Canada

*Miss Pauline M. Webb
Methodist Church, UK

Commissioner Harry W.
Williams
Salvation Army, UK

Ms A. Jean Woolfolk
Christian Church
(Disciples of Christ), USA

Rt Rev. Kenneth Woollcombe
Church of England

Ms Margaret A. Youngquist
American Lutheran Church

Mrs Jean Zaru
Friends United Meeting, Jordan

Prof. John Zizioulas
Ecumenical Patriarchate

Mrs Hildegard Zumach
Evangelical Church in Germany
United, FRG

APPENDIX XI

THE PERIODICALS OF THE WORLD COUNCIL

On a subscription basis

THE ECUMENICAL REVIEW: The quarterly journal of the WCC, in which the major theological, ethical and other issues relating to the work of the Council in particular and the ecumenical movement as a whole, are discussed and debated.

ECUMENICAL PRESS SERVICE: Aims at keeping its readers informed of trends of thought and opinion in and about the churches and Christian movements. Approximately 35 mailings a year (news bulletins, features and photos). Available also in French: "Service œcuménique de Presse et d'Information."

INTERNATIONAL REVIEW OF MISSION: The quarterly journal on mission and evangelism in six continents, published by the Commission on World Mission and Evangelism, which promotes study and discussion of all aspects of the church's mission. Published for over 60 years.

ONE WORLD: A popular, well-illustrated monthly magazine (published ten times a year) bringing first-hand information of general interest about the World Council and the churches around the world.

RISK: A book series published three times a year, each issue is devoted to exploring less well-covered ecumenical themes in greater detail. Well illustrated.

WCC EXCHANGE: A bi-monthly documentation service through which the churches exchange the actual texts of their statements and studies, rather than relying on second-hand reports.

Free of charge (any contributions towards costs of postage and printing are welcome)

ANTICIPATION: Published approximately three times a year by the sub-unit on Church and Society.

CCIA NEWSLETTER AND CCIA BACKGROUND INFORMATION: Two publications of the Commission of the Churches on International Affairs (approximately five times a year).

CCPD ACTIVITY REPORT: Published once a year by the Commission on the Churches' Participation in Development.

CCPD DOCUMENTS: A service of the development education research and documentation programme of CCPD. Two or three issues a year.

CCPD NETWORK LETTER: Published twice a year.

CHURCH ALERT: An ecumenical review of Christian social thought and action, published bi-monthly in conjunction with the Society, Development and Peace (SODEPAX) programme "In search of a new society".

THE CHURCH AND THE JEWISH PEOPLE: A quarterly newsletter of the sub-unit on Dialogue with People of Living Faiths and Ideologies.

CONTACT: A bi-monthly publication of the Christian Medical Commission. News from all over the world dealing with Christian communities' involvement in health care. Available in English, French, Spanish and Portuguese.

EDUCATION NEWSLETTER: A quarterly publication of the Office of Education.

JUSTICE AND SERVICE: Published twice a year by the Programme Unit II, "Justice and Service". Only available in French.

MIGRATION TODAY: Discusses current problems and Christian responsibility. Published annually by the Migrant Committee.

MINISTERIAL FORMATION: Encourages sharing and cooperation among all who are working for the renewal of the churches through programmes of ministerial formation. Published by the Programme on Theological Education.

MONTHLY LETTER ABOUT EVANGELISM: Published ten times a year by the Commission on World Mission and Evangelism.

NEWSLETTER: COMMUNITY OF WOMEN AND MEN IN THE CHURCH: Focuses on the implication for the churches of women's involvement in theology and ministry. Functions as a communication link between the various groups working on the study. Three issues a year.

WOMEN: A newsletter on the programme of the sub-unit on Women in the Church and Society, and on activities of women's groups in the WCC member churches.

YOUTH NEWSLETTER: Ecumenical and WCC youth news from all over the world. Published four times a year by the Youth Department.

84

APPENDIX XII
FOR FURTHER READING

ADLER, ELISABETH. *A Small Beginning*. Geneva: WCC, 1974, 102 pp.
An assessment of the first five years of the WCC's Programme to Combat Racism, what it has achieved, and what remains to be done.

ANDERSON, GERALD H. and THOMAS F. STRANSKY (eds.). *Mission Trends*. Nos. 1-3. New York: Paulist Press, and Grand Rapids: Eerdmans, 1974-1976, 3 vols.
A collection of valuable essays on crucial issues in mission evangelization and Third World theologies today.

BENT, A. J. VAN DER. *God So Loves the World: the Immaturity of World Christianity*. Madras: Christian Literature Society, 1977, 143 pp.
A critical examination of the credibility of worldwide Christian reflections and actions in the light (or rather, in the darkness) of Third World poverty and want, particularly in Calcutta, testing the Church's readiness and capacity to meet the modern multi-religious and secular world on its own ground.

BÜHLMANN, WALBERT. *The Coming of the Third Church: an Analysis of the Present and the Future of the Church*. Maryknoll, NY: Orbis Books, 1977, 419 pp.
The author, secretary general for the Capuchin missions throughout the world, sees the church's mission to humanity entering a new phase, one in which new questions are being asked (and radical answers given) because the situations in which people find themselves today cannot be handled along time-honoured lines. A very thought-provoking book.

EDWARDS, DAVID L. *The British Churches Turn to the Future*. London: SCM, 1973, 88 pp.
An evaluation of a church leaders' conference with a difference. Five hundred representatives of the British and Irish churches met in Birmingham for ten days in September 1972 not to legislate and pass on resolutions, but to join together in considering in depth the crises Christians are facing.

FEINER, JOHANNES and LUKAS VISCHER (eds.). *The Common Catechism: a Christian Book of Faith*. London: Search Press, and New York: Seabury Press, 1975, 690 pp.
A first common catechism or joint statement of Christian faith produced by Roman Catholics and Protestants since the separation of the churches in the 16th century. Translated and published in more than ten modern languages.

FEY, HAROLD E. (ed.). *The Ecumenical Advance: a History of the Ecumenical Movement, Vol. 2, 1948-1968*. London: SPCK, 1970, 524 pp.
The "official" history of the ecumenical movement and the World Council of Churches since its founding in 1948. Contains various contributions by World Council staff members and ecumenical theologians.

FOR ALL GOD'S PEOPLE: ECUMENICAL PRAYER CYCLE. Geneva: WCC, London: SPCK, and Madras: Christian Literature Society, 1978, 240 pp.
A guide assisting churches and Christians throughout the world in both public worship and private prayers of intercession for each

other. Responsibility for the project was borne primarily by the WCC's Faith and Order Commission and the sub-unit on Renewal and Congregational Life. Representatives from the Roman Catholic Church, the Lutheran World Federation and the World Alliance of Reformed Churches participated in the preparations.

GENTZ, WILLIAM H. *The World of Philip Potter*. New York: Friendship Press, 1974, 96 pp.
A short biography and evaluation of the background and experiences of the third general secretary of the World Council of Churches.

GOODALL, NORMAN. *Ecumenical Progress: a Decade of Change in the Ecumenical Movement, 1961-71*. London: Oxford University Press, 1972, 173 pp.
A sequel to his book *The Ecumenical Movement: What It Is and What It Does (1964)*. Brings together information not accessible in many other volumes. The author has been long associated with the World Council in several different capacities.

IN EACH PLACE. TOWARDS A FELLOWSHIP OF LOCAL CHURCHES TRULY UNITED. Geneva: WCC, 1977, 92 pp.
What precisely are the churches really looking for when they talk and pray for the unity of "all in each place"? What, practically, does such unity mean for the way local congregations in a particular area understand themselves and shape their common life? Some answers to these questions.

LANGE, ERNST. *And Yet It Moves: Dream and Reality of the Ecumenical Movement*. Belfast: Christian Journals Ltd., 1978, 192 pp.
A brilliant analysis of the strengths and weaknesses of the ecumenical movement and a personal account of the experience made in the service of the ecumenical cause.

MILLWOOD, DAVID. *The Poverty Makers*. Geneva: WCC Commission on the Churches' Participation in Development, 1977, 69 pp.
This material, intended for a non-specialist readership — people interested in the causes of poverty and injustice — is drawn from *Patterns of Poverty in the Third World* by Charles Elliott and Françoise de Morsier (New York: Praeger, 1975), which resulted from a three-year study of the prospects for the poorest fourth of the world's population.

MODERN EUCHARISTIC AGREEMENT. London: SPCK, 1973, 89 pp.
Provides useful material for discussion groups and those interested in recent ecumenical developments concerning statements on progress towards Christian unity through eucharistic communion.

ONE BAPTISM, ONE EUCHARIST AND A MUTUALLY RECOGNIZED MINISTRY. THREE AGREED STATEMENTS. Geneva: WCC, 1975, 65 pp.
The texts in this booklet are presented in the hope that they may help the churches to discover their oneness in fellowship with Christ and thus come to live together in unity.

THE ORTHODOX CHURCH IN THE ECUMENICAL MOVEMENT. DOCUMENTS AND STATEMENTS 1902-1975. Geneva: WCC, 1978, 350 pp.
An important documentary history of the presence and witness of the Orthodox Church at the centre of the ecumenical movement.

THE ORTHODOX CHURCH AND THE CHURCHES OF THE REFORMATION: A SURVEY OF ORTHODOX-PROTESTANT DIALOGUES. Faith and Order Paper No. 76. Geneva: WCC, 1975, 101 pp.
Contains accounts of various dialogues, a synoptic analysis and evaluation, and personal statements from ten Orthodox and Protestant theologians.

SAMARTHA, S. J. (ed.). *Faith in the Midst of Faiths: Reflections on Dialogue in Community*. Geneva: WCC, 1977, 200 pp.
Eighty-five Christians — Roman Catholic, Orthodox, Anglican and Protestant — came together in Chiang Mai, Thailand, in April 1977 to consider various questions and issues under the theme "Dialogue in Community". The meeting was sponsored by the WCC Sub-Unit on Dialogue with People of Living Faiths and Ideologies. The book contains Bible studies, papers and critical reflections.

SLACK, KENNETH. *Nairobi Narrative: the Story of the Fifth Assembly of the World Council of Churches, 23 November-10 December 1975*. London: SCM Press, 1976, 90 pp.
The author, a former general secretary of the British Council of Churches and now director of Christian Aid, describes the happenings of the vast gathering of church representatives in Nairobi late in 1975.

THE UNITY BOOK OF PRAYERS. London: Geoffrey Chapman, 1969, 119 pp.
A collection of familiar and unfamiliar prayers, for public and private use throughout the year, and especially during the Christian unity octave.

VISSER 'T HOOFT, W. A. *Has the Ecumenical Movement a Future?* Belfast: Christian Journals Limited, 1974, 97 pp.
A penetrating look by the first general secretary of the World Council of Churches at the ecumenical witness in the religious world, a crisp *tour de force* of the four periods of modern ecumenical history, and an assessment at a time of growing international criticism of the WCC.

VISSER 'T HOOFT, W. A. *Memoirs*. London: SCM Press, 1973, 379 pp.
An account of the experiences of the first general secretary of the World Council of Churches, who has been involved in international ecumenical life for more than fifty years.